WAR AND PEACE

Tolstoy's Mirror of the World

TWAYNE'S MASTERWORK STUDIES

Robert Lecker, General Editor

WAR AND PEACE

Tolstoy's Mirror of the World

Rimvydas Silbajoris

TWAYNE PUBLISHERS
An Imprint of Simon & Schuster Macmillan
New York

PRENTICE HALL INTERNATIONAL
London • Mexico City • New Delhi • Singapore • Sydney • Toronto

Twayne's Masterwork Series No. 146

War and Peace: Tolstoy's Mirror of the World
Rimvydas Šilbajoris

Copyright © 1995 by Twayne Publishers

Twayne Publishers
An Imprint of Simon & Schuster Macmillan
866 Third Avenue
New York, New York 10022

Library of Congress Cataloging-in-Publication Data

Šilbajoris, Rimvydas, 1926–
    War and peace : Tolstoy's mirror of the world / Rimvydas Šilbajoris
        p.   cm.—(Twayne's masterwork studies ; no. 146)
    Includes bibliographical references and index.
    ISBN 0-8057-9449-2 (cloth).—ISBN 0-8057-4459-2 (pbk.)
    1. Tolstoy, Leo, graf, 1828–1910. Voĭna i mir.   I. Title.   II. Series.
PG3365.V65S53   1995
891.73'3—dc20   95-2950
                                                                                 CIP

10 9 8 7 6 5 4 3 2 1 (hc)
10 9 8 7 6 5 4 3 2 1 (pb)

Printed in the United States of America

Contents

Note on the References and Acknowledgments   *vii*
Chronology: Lev Tolstoy's Life and Works   *ix*

LITERARY AND HISTORICAL CONTEXT
   1. Tolstoy's Russia: Between East and West   3
   2. *War and Peace:* The Towering Novel   9
   3. Kicking the Mountain: The Critics' Response   15

A READING
   4. Conception and Growth of the Novel   29
   5. The World of Perceptions   39
   6. Perspectives: Author, Reader, Character   55
   7. Recurrences and Linkages   74
   8. Dynamics and Building Blocks   92
   9. Genre and the Hero   108

Notes and References   *125*
Bibliography   *141*
Index   *145*

Leo Tolstoy, about 1885.

Note on the References and Acknowledgments

All references in the text to Lev Nikolaevich Tolstoy's *War and Peace* are from the Aylmer Maude translation, George Gibian, editor (New York: Norton, 1966), and are cited parenthetically as *W&P*. Some of the critical works referred to are in Russian; translations of their titles are provided in parentheses immediately following the original, and any quotes from them are given in English. Translations of the titles are my own.

This essay is one more try, among many made before by others, to provide sufficient insight into both Tolstoy's epic novel and some basic features of his artistic method, as well as to stimulate interest in reading the book. Tolstoy himself has made sure that readers who unfold its pages will be opening the door to a tremendously rich and beautiful universe of thought and feeling that they will never want to leave, wherever their walks of life might take them.

Having walked humbly with Lev Nikolaevich for a number of years, I met many people, some only through their books, others personally, who loved him, and a few who did not. I feel I owe them all a debt of gratitude too enormous ever to repay. Among my colleagues in the Slavic field, some particularly stand out: Professor Victor Terras of Brown, who has been my mentor because he taught me to have affection for Tolstoy's work and clarity of thought regarding it; Professor Richard Edgerton of Indiana, from whom I learned persistence and enduring enthusiasm for work; and perhaps most of all Professor Gary

Saul Morson of Northwestern, who I thank for his warm human contact and invaluable, sparkling personal thoughts about the mystery of Tolstoy's genius. He also has taught me that thinking can be fun. Most particularly, I also wish to thank the participants in my NEH Summer Seminars for Teachers in 1983, 1984, and 1986. Many of the ideas about *War and Peace* were germinated and brought to fruition with their help during our intense, lively, wonderful discussions.

Thanks go to the Slavic Department at Ohio State, where I always have found support, and personally, to my wife, Milda, a tower of strength and patience through all of this.

Chronology: Lev Tolstoy's Life and Works

1828   Lev Nikolaevich Tolstoy born 9 September on his father's estate, Yasnaya Polyana, near Tula, south of Moscow.

1830   Tolstoy's mother dies, followed by his father in 1837. Tolstoy is brought up by an aunt.

1844   Enters the University of Kazan; first studies oriental languages, then law.

1847   Leaves the University of Kazan without graduating. Leads an aimless, dissipated life in Petersburg and Moscow, as well as on his Yasnaya Polyana estate.

1851   Goes to the Caucasus; obtains commission in the army. Participates in skirmishes with mountain tribespeople.

1852   Completes *Childhood*, published in *Sovremennik* (The Contemporary), a leading literary journal. It is the first part of a quasi-autobiographic trilogy, the other two parts being *Adolescence* (1854) and *Youth* (1857).

1853   Serves with the Army of the Danube at the outbreak of the Russo-Turkish War.

1854   Participates as an artillery officer in the defense of Sevastopol during the Crimean War (1854–56) against Britain, Turkey, and France. Stalwart at his post, Tolstoy nevertheless conceives a deep revulsion of war and the trappings of the military life.

1855   Leaves the army; goes to Petersburg as a young writer famous for his *Sevastopol' Sketches* (1855–56), a set of essays of ostensibly journalistic intent that nevertheless contain many of the most important seeds of Tolstoy's later prose. Finds the literary ambience in Petersburg uncongenial and full of empty chatter. Withdraws to Yasnaya Polyana and renounces art as just another sort of empty talk, a "beautiful lie."

1857
Briefly visits Western Europe. Witnesses a public execution in Paris, which reinforces his already nagging doubts about the values and achievements of Western civilization. For the next few years he remains in Yasnaya Polyana and struggles through an inner crisis that challenges the entire traditional system of values, including those of art, which has been inculcated in him by virtue of his status in society.

1860–1861
Makes a more extensive visit to Western Europe for the main purpose of studying firsthand the European systems of education. Tolstoy is disappointed to see European education as a system of suppression and intimidation intended not to educate children, but to force them to accept mindlessly the dominant, and in his opinion, false standards of society.

1861
Tolstoy's brother Nikolay dies of tuberculosis. This leads Tolstoy to dark contemplations on death, which later enter the realm of his art and find a crucial function in *War and Peace* (in the death of Prince Andrey Bolkonsky), *Anna Karenina* (in the death of Konstantin Levin's brother), and in the harrowing story *The Death of Ivan Ilyich*.

1862–1863
While teaching peasant children, publishes a journal called *Not•s from Yasnaya Polyana*, where he expounds decidedly unconventional ideas about education that are permeated with Rousseauistic thoughts on the dignity of the natural man and the joy of spontaneous, unregimented learning. Exercises in story writing convince Tolstoy that these children, filled with genuine emotion and an instinctive but profound and subtle feeling for truth, can produce fiction superior to that of the world's most famous artists.

1862
Marries Sofya Andreevna Behrs, a neighbor. Begins a family life fruitful in children and artistic works, one that later becomes stormy and torturous due to the incompatibility of the personalities of Tolstoy and his wife and of their ideas pertaining to the values of society.

1863
The Cossacks published. It is the story of a city-bred officer in search of a truthful and happy way of life among "nature's children," the Cossacks, in a military settlement along the Terek River at the foothills of the Caucasian Mountains.

1863–1869
Writes *War and Peace*. A grand story of epic scope, it intertwines the destinies of many real and invented people during Russia's "Napoleonic Wars," which start in 1805 and end with Napoleon's crushing defeat in 1812. Parts of the novel appeared serially in the journal *The Russian Messenger* from

Chronology

1865 to 1866. Later the journal published the novel again in six separate volumes: volumes 1 through 3 in 1867; volume 4 in 1868; and volumes 5 and 6 in 1869. After various revisions it was published once more in 1873.

1869–1873   Devotes his time to pedagogical work, producing *A New Primer* and *A Russian Reader*, both published in 1875.

1877   Publishes *Anna Karenina*. A tale of unhappy marriage and illicit, unhappy love alongside another story of love and marriage in which a plateau of happiness is attained. These events unfold against the troubled background of Russia in a time of change, with urban, industrial, and mercantile values displacing an agricultural way of life, one dominated by landed aristocracy.

1870–1880   Produces much religious and moral writing, but little artistic work. This period is Tolstoy's second abandonment of his art, an action motivated by his concerns over crushing poverty and moral decay in Russia and the Western world. These concerns are most compellingly stated in his 1882 essay, "So What Are We Then to Do?"

1882   *A Confession* is published. The work describes Tolstoy's religious doubts, intellectual despair, and conversion to a simple faith, one similar, he believes, to that of the peasants who, innocent of philosophy, listen to the voice of God in their hearts.

1886   Publishes *The Death of Ivan Ilyich*, the story of a typical Russian bourgeois, by profession a judge and by his own conviction a decent fellow, who learns through the relentless agony of his illness and death that his former "ordinary" life had actually been morally rotten and terrible.

1890   Publishes *The Kreutzer Sonata*, a marital tale of, in order, music, jealousy, and death, in which Tolstoy openly expresses his increasing revulsion toward carnal sex and even the institution of marriage.

1891   Organizes relief activities in response to a famine caused by crop failures in central and southeastern Russia. Tolstoy's critical, accusatory views on the causes of the famine, marriage, religion, and on the oppressive policies of the ruling classes and their government set the Russian authorities against him. Yet they do not allow him to become their direct political victim, preferring instead to persecute and punish his followers.

1904   Publishes *Hadji Murat*, a brilliantly written story about a Caucasian tribal leader who fights Russian oppression to his very death.

1897   *What Is Art?*, a summary of Tolstoy's esthetics, is published. Highly unorthodox and iconoclastic, Tolstoy's views discount as false most of the art produced in the history of Western cultural tradition. Tolstoy maintains that art evolves not from the use of artifice, but from direct emotional communication.

1899   *The Resurrection* is published. The work describes a spoiled, rich landowner who becomes conscience-stricken at the wrongful sentencing of a woman he had once seduced, and who he decides to follow all the way to Siberia in order to expiate his own guilt.

1901   Tolstoy is excommunicated from the Russian Orthodox church for his religious articles, which reject all the basic tenets of its teaching.

1910   In October Tolstoy leaves Yasnaya Polyana to escape his intolerable family situation. Tolstoy dies on 22 November in the small railroad station of Astapovo.

LITERARY AND
HISTORICAL CONTEXT

1

Tolstoy's Russia:
Between East and West

In the beginning of his life, Lev Tolstoy was a typical Russian provincial aristocrat. Surrounded by laboring serfs, he lived in leisure, and with no obligations to anyone, on a comfortable estate. His ambition was to serve his country as a soldier, in a manner worthy of his privileged, aristocratic class. In its real-life origins, the novel *War and Peace* rests on the foundations of two realities in Tolstoy's personal life: participation in the Crimean War, and peace in his early, happy days in Yasnaya Polyana.[1]

It is difficult to speak of significant outside influences on Tolstoy's novel. His work is very much his own and basically stands apart from both Russian and Western literary traditions of the time. Tolstoy insisted that *War and Peace* was not a novel in any conventional sense, and even implied that it should not be read as "literature," that is, as mere entertainment, but as something else altogether—an articulation of the epic majesty of life when it is lived fully. Nonetheless, an author's thoughts are not an isolated shaft of light piercing the void and making sense of it. Instead, what the reader actually experiences is an ongoing relationship between the creative idea and the personal, cultural, and historical context in which it is placed.

The most important ideological crosscurrents in nineteenth-century Russia belonged to the so-called Westernizers and Slavophiles. The westernizing movement had its roots in the seventeenth century, following the "time of troubles," the invasion of Russia by Poland-Lithuania, during which many ideas and customs of the Catholic West spread throughout Russia. This influence was strengthened when, under the Empress Catherine II (1762–96), Russia gained the territories of the Ukraine and Byelorussia, both of which under the previous Polish rule had developed a number of Western-style cultural and social institutions. Catherine herself corresponded with and drew to her court the famous French intellectuals of the time, including the encyclopedist Denis Diderot,[2] and tried to promulgate humanistic learning and liberal reforms in the governance of the empire. Some Russians became painfully aware that traditionally they had been different from Western Europe, that is, from the entire powerful growth of modern civilization initiated by the dawning of the New Age around 1492, and so they began to develop a Western-oriented mode of thought in the hope of bringing their country up to par with the West.

Tsar Peter I (1672–1725) undertook very vigorous and sweeping reforms, jolting the old Russia of the bojars (members of the landed gentry) into modern times, often with considerable violence. His main interest was in the military, technical, and economic progress of the country, for which purposes he enlisted skilled Westerners (Germans, Scots, the Dutch, and Italians) to help with his projects. In the eighteenth century, "Russia submitted with amazing wholeheartedness to the cultural values, myths, prejudices, and even objects emanating from France and elsewhere in Europe,"[3] and almost simultaneously its literature went through several Western movements that had taken some two or three centuries to develop, and that Russia had missed altogether, such as classicism, baroque, rococo, sentimentalism, and even romanticism.

After the Napoleonic Wars this orientation was much strengthened by some intellectuals cum officers in the Russian army who had marched into Paris in 1825 and seen the Western mode of life in

Europe. Dreams of a constitutional monarchy and of the further westernization of Russia led to the failed Decembrist revolt,[4] after which the traditional, conservative tsarist autocracy reasserted itself with crushing force. Pierre Bezukhov, the main hero of *War and Peace*, was originally conceived by Tolstoy as a Decembrist returned from exile. Thus the story of his ideological development includes the seminal force of all the Western ideas that sprung up in Russia before, during, and after the Napoleonic Wars. In real life, the westward-looking philosophy remained in the minds of many of the Russian intelligentsia even after the Decembrist disaster, and eventually it became an ideology representing liberal, progressive, rationalistic, and sometimes even socialist-utopian views. This Western trend of thought produced some of Russia's most influential literary critics and social commentators of the time. Among the former were Vissarion Belinsky (1811–44), Nikolai Chernyshevsky (1828–89), and Nikolai Dobrolyubov (1836–61), all of whose work laid the foundation underlying the socially and politically oriented mode of Russian literary discourse that in a number of ways retains its influence in the present day. Notable among the Russian social thinkers was Alexander Herzen (1812–70), whose influence became especially strong after 1847, the year he was forced into exile and during which he wrote for and edited two famous publications, the journals the *Northern Star* and the newspaper the *Bell*, depositories of liberal, at times even implicitly revolutionary ideas, which engaged many young Russian intellectuals. In belles lettres, perhaps the most famous of the "Westernizers" was Ivan Turgenev (1818–83), who had drunk deeply of Western cultures, especially those of the Germans and the French, and who expounded rational liberalism in all of his works.

Although attracted by the humanistic liberalism of the Westernizers, Tolstoy on the whole did not trust their mode of thought, just as he mistrusted and even opposed the entire edifice of Western civilization. In *War and Peace* we see this mistrust in the negative portrayals of Napoleon and other military leaders, whom Tolstoy shows as representing the Western penchant for rationalistic theorizing and model-building.[5] We also see his anti-Westernism in Tolstoy's views of history, which he expressed throughout the novel in both expository argument and the portrayal of characters' destinies, as a pattern of random configurations of actions that stem from an impulse at the given moment; this view is in contrast to the logical causality in human affairs that served as the norm for a well-written novel in the West.

This preference for the organic and instinctive principle in life brings Tolstoy somewhat closer to Slavophilism, which arose as an articulated school of thought in the nineteenth century, but which, in its remote origins, goes back to the ways of Old Russia, as imagined at that time through nostalgic illusion. In the eighteenth century, nationalistic reaction against "gallomania" from the West tended to be shared by liberal and conservative thinkers alike. It can be seen, for instance, in the fables of Ivan Krylov (1769–1844), a shrewd, talented archconservative with a sense of humor and a love for freedom, as well as in the satirical journalism of Nikolay Novikov (1744–1818), a Freemason and bold opponent of the increasing autocracy and intellectual pretensions of Catherine II. In time, the resentment toward foreign influences on the Russian lifestyle turned to hostility toward the Russian state, and especially its leader, Peter I, because of his implementation of Western reforms.

In the 1830s the distinctly Slavophilic point of view was formulated by the Russian intellectuals and journalists Ivan Kireevsky (1806–56), Aleksey Khomyakov (1804–60), and Konstantin Aksakov (1817–60). Among their basic tenets was the belief that the Russian nation possessed unique qualities of deep and humble humanity; chief among these was the ability to perceive society, which consisted of the people, the church, and the state, as bound together by the values and emotions of a great and intimate family. These qualities pointed the way to a historical development in which it was asserted that the Russian people did not need to and should not follow any Western models. Quite the contrary—it was believed that because of their special qualities, the Russian people could become the source of inspiration and salvation for the entire human race. Such messianistic ideas, embedded first and foremost in the concept of a special destiny for the Russian people, were promulgated by the most important Russian writers of the nineteenth century. The great Russian novelist Fyodor

Dostoyevski (1821–81) especially articulated them in his last novel, *The Brothers Karamazov*, as did Nikolay Gogol (1809–52) in his *Passages from a Correspondence with Friends*.

The Slavophiles spoke for the spontaneity of the "broad Russian nature" and saw great powers and profound spiritual strength in the common Russian peasants and in their way of life, which was based on community values closely tied to the communal spirit of the traditional Russian church. Tolstoy also deeply respected the common people. In fact, *War and Peace* is in many ways an apotheosis of their great Russian spirit. Nevertheless, he did not share the Slavophiles' messianic mysticism of a "holy Russia," nor did he approve of the Russian imperialism that in part arose from such romantic and mystic notions.

Against the background of this Westernizer-Slavophile dichotomy, the tsarist government asserted its right to speak about philosophic and moral value systems that it viewed as obligatory for the subjects of the empire. Its peremptory voice in essence denied the legitimacy, indeed permissibility, of any other modes of thought on the implicitly and sometimes almost explicitly stated grounds that the ordinary person had no business seeking any other legal, intellectual, or moral relationship with the Russian state and church except that of obedience to it. The views of the state were most vigorously articulated by Konstantin Pobedonostsev (1827–1907), tutor to Tsar Alexander III and procurator of the Holy Synod. At the core of his political worldview was the firm belief in autocracy, orthodoxy, and Russian nationalism as the governing principles of the Russian state and nation. He was especially vociferous in his denunciations of Western rationalism and liberalism. Pobedonostsev's views in part coincided with those of the Slavophiles, except that the willingness of the Russian state to absorb the Western developments in bureaucracy and technology, that is, its acceptance of a soulless, formal view of the body politic of the nation, was a concept that was quite alien to the Slavophiles. Conversely, the interest in exploiting science and technology for Russian needs accommodated the desires of the Westernizers, yet they decidedly rejected the entire autocratic-religious edifice of state authority, as well as its political imperialism, an outgrowth in part of the messianic ideas of the Russian Slavophiles.[6]

Tolstoy's *War and Peace* is set years before Pobedonostsev and the entire Westernizer-Slavophile controversy; nevertheless, it transplants some of these issues into its own time frame, transforming them in the process. Tolstoy oriented the novel's Westernizers toward Europe, as distinguished from Russia. He portrayed them as high Russian aristocracy, people who spoke French among themselves and never gave a moment's thought to the rest of the country, except as a source of income. These people were very "Western" indeed, and yet very traditionally Russian in their silken cocoon of isolation; one irony in the novel is that the Russian masses, who stood up against Napoleon, by extension defended this seemingly alienated aristocracy as well. The Slavophiles' exalted mysticism about the depths of the Russian soul became emphatically demythologized when translated into the plain human bravery of such characters as the sweaty, not-too-bright, red-nosed Russian officer Captain Tushin at Schöngraben; or the peasants at Borodino; or, finally, the smelly, round peasant Karataev, who instinctively knew the right way to live without being able to put a grammatical sentence together. Confronted with the challenge of war, such people became united with other Russians, of all kinds and from all walks of life, to become a single entity facing the invader. As the Russian scholar S. Bocharov points out,[7] the Napoleonic Wars were quite a different war experience, for because of them, what was once a society with long-established social conventions became a community, the Russian *mir*—a word meaning both *world* and *peace*, as well as a peasant community of self-government, a social-administrative and spiritual institution. This term, *mir*, is the second word in the book's title, and its meaning is much more complex than the mere notion of peace.

2

War and Peace:
The Towering Novel

To perceive how unique Tolstoy's novel appeared to his contemporary readers, one only needs to set it beside other Russian works of this genre in the nineteenth century. When Tolstoy began *War and Peace* in 1863, Russian prose could already boast of several major figures, such as Nikolay Gogol, author of *Dead Souls* (1842), a tragicomic novel-poem about Russian provincial life; Fyodor Dostoyevski, whose heroes were servants of God even as they opposed him in such novels as *Crime and Punishment* (1866) and *The Brothers Karamazov* (1880); Ivan Turgenev, a poignant storyteller of the Russian countryside in his *Notes of a Hunter* (1852) and a chronicler of the conflict of generations in the novel *Fathers and Sons* (1862); and Ivan Goncharov (1812–91), whose bedside novel *Oblomov* (1859) carefully recorded the idle, dreamy lives of the decaying Russian landowning class.

One fundamental difference between these novels and Tolstoy's is the latter's broad epic sweep, which covers events of many years across enormous spaces and involves many life stories, both real and invented. Tolstoy's other radical departure from the conventions of the genre has to do with the dimension of time itself. Although some of the works just mentioned were contemporary with *War and Peace* and others preceded or followed it by some years, they all were set in their authors' own time frames. Tolstoy's novel is different in that while it is set in the past, the lives of his fictional characters, the various particular, private scenes and events, the movements, glances, habits, customs, perceptions, together with their social and cultural ambiance, are to a considerable extent drawn from directly experienced and vividly remembered details of Tolstoy's own life. We find ourselves in a world of superimposed time frames, one in which Pierre Bezukhov's or Nikolay Rostov's epic Russia of 1812 is combined with those characters' personal, intimate modes of being, an aspect of the aforementioned outstanding mid-century Russian novels. As we observe this astonishing juxtaposition, Tolstoy's novel becomes enriched with one more dimension, next to those of history, philosophy, and a complex fictional plot—namely, that in which two eras of history have come together.

Other ties also existed between Tolstoy and other Russian and foreign writers. For instance, the Russian critic A. Saburov says Tolstoy could have learned from Aleksandr Pushkin's tale *The Captain's Daughter*, which deals with the vast uprising of the Cossack leader Pugachev against Catherine II, how to produce a text obliterating the dividing line between the fictional and the historical.[1] Some other scholars have expressed the credible opinion that in depicting his war scenes as chaotic and irrational, Tolstoy may have learned from Stendahl's *The Charterhouse of Parma*. Tolstoy was also not altogether alone in the realm of ideas. As the Russian formalist critic Boris Eikhenbaum (1886–1959) points out, the issues of individual freedom versus determinism, and of causality in history, both of which are so important in the novel, were very much under discussion in Russia during the 1860s.[2] Eikhenbaum further contends that Tolstoy's negative portrait of Napoleon resembles that painted by the French journalist Pierre Proudhon and that Prince Andrey's conviction—so close to Tolstoy's own—that there is no art or science to war, may also have its roots in Proudhon. Other influences may have been the Russian historian Mikhail P. Pogodin, and the Slavophile mathematician and thinker Sergei S. Urusov, whose views on causality and on freedom and necessity are similar to Tolstoy's arguments in the novel. Nevertheless, the presence of all these native and foreign influences in the novel do not constitute a sum of its parts—they are nothing but references, points of contact, raw materials for the work, which stands on its own.

Tolstoy's place in this impressive company of thinkers and artists may be approached from two directions. One will take us across a somewhat misty rhetorical landscape where the attributes of *War and Peace*'s greatness, their heights shrouded in a verbal fog, may at times appear larger than they are. Tolstoy's friend and translator Aylmer Maude made one of the most succinct statements of this sort about the novel:

> *War and Peace* presents us with a complete picture of human life; a complete picture of the Russia of those days; a complete picture of the struggle of nations; and a complete picture of the things in which men set their happiness and greatness, their sorrow and their shame. It is a work so amazingly great that though many have *felt* its greatness, few have *understood* how great it is. Tolstoy is one who reveals the secrets of life and death. The meaning of history, the strength of nations, the mystery of death, the reality of love and family life—such are the subjects he deals with.[3]

In our own time, similarly intense high praise is heard from many corners. However, the greatness the critics are discussing—the universality of Tolstoy's work, his deep humanity, his grand epic sweep, his profound moral message—does not in itself explain the qualities of his art. Indeed, the more criticism one reads, the more it becomes apparent that what is under consideration is not literature (something that is ultimately only about itself), but life in its totality. Commentators on the novel are asking us not to regard it as an outstanding piece of artifice, but as the great book of life; that is, not as a reflection or articulation but as life itself; not as fiction, but as a universe parallel to the one in which we live. From this perspective, Tolstoy's achievement looms large in the eyes of many readers as the greatest word ever spoken by the Russian nation and as one of the most important spiritual forces in all humanity. However, such high distinction could be achieved by an outstanding historian, a noble moral leader, a profound philosopher, or a great lover of humanity, even if he or she were not an artist at all. Tolstoy's novel, however, in spite of the elaborate historical-philosophical arguments toward its end, does not seek to prove any particular "truths."[4] Instead, the novel is focused intensely upon the infinite possibilities of harmonious relationships and mutual enrichment of its many different component parts, where a blade of grass, a kernel of thought, the enormity of events, and a brief look of love are entities of the same order and function, a means to the creation of an enormous artistic totality, a world of its own (Bocharov, 10).

In 1851 the young Tolstoy wrote in his diary: "Imagination is a mirror of nature which we carry in ourselves and in which it paints itself. The most beautiful imagination is the clearest and most truthful mirror, the one we call a genius. A genius does not create, it retraces."[5] At the time he may have actually believed art was a matter of mimesis, the more accurate the better, but as we read his entire work, we begin to see that this is not the case. What Tolstoy actually has done is retrace the design of "nature" to its minutest detail, but with a magic pen, a pen that makes every line which in nature is merely "there" into a signifier of many complex experiences, arguments, ideas, and images originating from the artist's mind, which has, in turn, absorbed the artist's perceived and imagined realities. The more accurate in its minute details of fact and feeling, and the complex interconnections between them, then the richer the magic line the artist has traced, and the more it achieves the quality of greatness from inert reality.

Consequently, there is something in *War and Peace* that insistently moves us to perceive the work not only as a realistic pictorial representation of the world, but also as a statement of high philosophical and moral order. Such a feeling rises up to us from the printed page as an attribute of the narrative discourse itself rather than as an ideological burdened imposed upon it. For this reason, an analysis of Tolstoy's ideas as we encounter them in *War and Peace* amounts to a contemplation of the novel's artistic qualities, which show themselves to be a set of value judgments about life, beyond the scope of narration, and which come from a dimension outside of art. We might say that if the world of outside realities, when carefully retraced by Tolstoy, becomes one of inner human experiences, then the world of ideas, retraced with equal care from its outlines in Tolstoy's mind, becomes the physical world of objects, movements, colors, and events. Thus, for instance, the morning mist that the Russian troops descend into just before the Battle of Austerlitz becomes the idea that all is lost, or the earth, shuddering under the blow of a cannonball slapping into the ground, also becomes the human agony of a soldier being flogged, naked and spreadeagled, on the grass. That is the second direction from which we may approach an assessment of Tolstoy's place in world literature, and in particular, in *War and Peace*.

Let us, as an example, consider Tolstoy's universality. He does not give us "a complete picture of human life," as Maude thought, but he creates the illusion that he does by showing us but a few basic objects, actions, and emotions in their endless modulations, embodiments, and recurrences. Death, for instance, pushes its way in through a closed door, comes carrying a candle, attends at human birth, turns into a gray lofty sky, spins in front of us like an artillery shell, and breaks off like an unfinished sentence. Similar long lists could be compiled for the many faces of love, the physical sensations of the body, and so on. One might say of Tolstoy that his soul yearned for the body[6]; in the novel, a great deal depends on the immediate palpability of things described, and on the real smell of death and the visceral delight in life, both of which he knew so well.

In our own existence all these recurrent experiences become in time but a gray mass that slips through the fingers of memory and brings little relevance to our present or future. Tolstoy kept all these disparate recurrences vibrantly relevant to and connected with each other, as if they were the many themes and variations in a large symphony. If in life a large number of half-forgotten recurrent events can gradually accumulate to a faint outline of meaning, Tolstoy can reproduce this process as well, and turn it into a lucid and dramatic presentation of history. In the novel, whenever we recognize that a person's experience is a recurrent modality of his own or other people's past life events, we also gain an insight into life as a whole. Thus Tolstoy makes our own real lives important to us through the perceptions of his imaginary characters. We may, for instance, consider the slow transition of Prince Andrey from his life of tumult and striving to his cosmic indifference toward death. The process is described for us in such a compelling way that as we see how he releases detail after detail of his own self, and returns to the nameless vastness of Being, it gradually dawns on us that this process is a movement of grace, a gesture of love for that encompassing perfect vastness. It is then that we ourselves gratefully perceive our own intense experience of being alive, instead of fearing death. It is a profound Tolstoyan paradox that as we, through Andrey's feelings, come to assent to death with increasing affection, we also learn more and more deeply "to love life in all its innumerable, inexhaustible manifestations," as Tolstoy said in describing the purpose of his own novel (*W&P*, 1360).

All things considered, *War and Peace* must be counted as the supreme achievement of Tolstoy's art, for it contains in a fuller, grander measure all the qualities of his genius, and all the power of his other works. While his other stories or novels deal in great profundity with particular aspects and issues of human life, for instance, marital fidelity in *Anna Karenina* (1877) and *Kreutzer Sonata* (1889), or the confrontation with death in *Death of Ivan Ilyich*, the novel *War and Peace* encompasses multiple aspects of life in a huge epic sweep, a wide-screen panorama of history as a presence in the human soul, and of the human soul as the fulfillment of history.

3

Kicking the Mountain: The Critics' Response

What critics have said about *War and Peace* could make another epic, one even larger and more complex than the novel itself, just as full of fact and fiction, and reflecting in its own mirror the entire panorama of European cultural history, from Tolstoy's day to our own. Tolstoy himself, of course, was also a reader of his novel and had his own opinions about it. Among the most helpful are his statements pertaining to the genre and the governing idea of the work. He set himself squarely against those who thought of art as just another means of resolving contemporary social or ideological issues. "The goals of art," said Tolstoy, "are incommensurate (as the mathematicians say) with social goals"[1] or with those of science, because instead of proving something objectively, his aim as author is to make us love life. Such a stance is useless to a professional critic,[2] for it fits none of his or her terminological or methodological categories, but to the reader it does make plain that the novel's aim, its basic idea, is to achieve a sharing of emotion with the reader about life as we know it, and life, to Tolstoy, was a great and wonderful thing. It is important for us as readers to sustain this understanding of Tolstoy's purpose and perceive the intensity of his feeling even as we hear him expound in a detached expository voice about free will, determinism, and the laws of history.

As to genre, Tolstoy admitted he was afraid that his writing "would fall into no existing genre, neither novel, nor tale, nor long poem, nor history" (W&P, 1363). The point is that genre distinctions describe various conventional modes of telling a story, and while the love for life Tolstoy wished to communicate could be called epic in its boundless generosity, it is not in itself a narration and thus could not become subordinate to storytelling rules. War and Peace does contain elements of almost every known genre, and it does tell quite a tale, but the fullness of life itself is free from time, space, and any sequencing of events. Consequently, in the end Tolstoy was forced to make a plain yet hermetical statement that permits neither analysis nor evaluation: "War and Peace is what the author wished and was able to express in the form in which it is expressed."[3] Tolstoy's critics, however, were not satisfied.

Some of the early critical voices accused Tolstoy of lacking that which he said his work was not meant to contain—a commitment to some social or philosophical idea. Tolstoy allegedly scattered himself in meaningless descriptive details, which lacked an ultimate coherence.[4] The fact that he did not consistently conform to any known genre conventions increased the confusion. Some assumed Tolstoy to have but limited education, which led to his purportedly primitive, negative outlook upon the civilized world. His fellow writer, Ivan Turgenev, whose esthetics were deeply rooted in the West, found much to criticize in the novel. Tolstoy's finely tuned psychological observations seemed to him trite and boring, dug out, under the pretense of "truth," from "under the armpits and other dark places of his characters,"[5] and Tolstoy's love of detail struck Turgenev as a mere hindrance to the large historical panorama that should have revealed the greatness of Russia in its time of trial.[6] From the very beginning there were readers who felt that Tolstoy did not mean to create glorious and epic visions of the Russian past, nor sustain the legend of it that already existed; rather, they believed he was bent on destroying, debunking, and belittling all that made up the historical greatness of Mother Russia. Boris Eikhenbaum reports on two critics, Shchebal'sky and Demenkov, the first of whom thought that accusations against Tolstoy for criticizing Kutuzov and Napoleon should have gone further: "We cannot agree that he [Tolstoy] supposedly just denies the glory of 1812 and belittles the merits of the Russian army. It seems to us that Count Tolstoy has a negative attitude *to everything*, that he is trying to destroy everything. He rejects Napoleon and Kutuzov, historical figures and the masses of the people, personal choice and the meaning of historical events. Possibly even without suspecting it, he brought a total, complete nihilism to history" (Eikhenbaum II, 391). The second critic sees the novel as "malicious parody, a viciously satirical story" and a "chaotic and anti-patriotic fairy-tale" (Eikhenbaum II, 390). Among such voices, only the poet Afanasy Fet tried if not to defend, then at least to understand what Tolstoy was doing, and wrote in 1866: "I understand that the main task of the novel is to turn an historical event inside out and look not at the official, gold-embroidered side of the dressing-gown, but at the chemise, the shirt, which is *closer to the body*."[7] Fet's commentary is rather perspicacious, at least in that he spoke of a particular principle, a particular manner on the basis of which the novel was built.

Tolstoy's belief that one should "love life in all its manifestations" almost seems to imply that life is an entity unto itself, different from particular living things, even as it manifests itself in them. Some Hegelian Russian critics, known as "organic" thinkers, also had similar notions. Notable among them was Nikolai N. Strakhov (1828–96), who believed life is a force that penetrates and passes through matter, and in this rush transforms it and brings forth actual living things. Strakhov perceived some analogous processes in *War and Peace*, in which Tolstoy simply and directly allows life to flood his created worlds instead of imposing upon them shapes descended from literary conventions that would pretend to be imitations of life. Therefore, according to Strakhov, Tolstoy was the supreme realist, and also uniquely Russian in that he created a special Russian literary genre "that rose from the depths of national life and reflected reality in more than rational aspects."[8]

The relationship between art and life was of particular interest to the civic-minded radical critics, of whom Nikolay Chernyshevsky

(1828–89) was thought to have some affinities of mind with Tolstoy, particularly in the generally held view that for both of them any criteria for evaluating art must come from outside of it, from some utilitarian purpose or, in Tolstoy's case, moral principle. Tolstoy, nevertheless, was as remote from practical aims in art as he was from "proving" anything by it. A utilitarian purpose, for instance, might be the use of art to affect human institutions, such as the improvement of the court system, or for equitable distribution of land, or for pacifism. Tolstoy, on the other hand, was speaking from a different dimension. From his art emerged the notions that no one should ever judge another human being, that land always and automatically belongs to everyone, and that life is not, or should not be, self-destructive in its essence. Fyodor Dostoyevski, author of many crime stories elevated to greatness by depth of thought, noticed particularly well Tolstoy's point in *Anna Karenina* that we are not to judge, because to do so requires the full knowledge of *all* the factors that went into a particular act, and such knowledge has only He who said "vengeance is mine and I shall repay."[9]

Actually, Chernyshevsky's most interesting remarks pertain to Tolstoy's technique of pervasive psychological analysis. Tolstoy, he said, is interested in the psychological process as such, the "dialectic of the mind." Tolstoy's attention

> is turned above all to the way in which one complex of thought-feelings derives from another. He is interested in observing how an emotion, arisen spontaneously from a given situation or impression, submits to the influence of memories and to the force of new relationships with them suggested by the imagination, becomes transformed into other thought-feelings, returns again to its point of departure, and wanders on and on, constantly changing, along the entire chain of recollections; how a primary thought leads to other thoughts, how it gets carried away more and more, and how it blends dreams with real sensations and daydreams of the future with reflections upon the present.[10]

Although written about Tolstoy's early work, this perception proves itself over and over again when one reads *War and Peace* and serves as a good guide through the novel's psychological complexities.

N. K. Mikhailovsky (1842–1904), the leading spokesman of the liberal Populists, found in Tolstoy two basic impulses constantly at war with each other: the rational principle, often applied by Tolstoy to his art, and a powerful irrational drive that penetrated Tolstoy's nonfictional writings, causing him to proclaim strange convictions based on misshapen logic. Tolstoy was at his best when his intellect and intuition were in harmonious balance, for then he produced outstanding works of art, like *War and Peace*. When the inner link between them was broken, they became mutually destructive, and it was as if Tolstoy had split into two individuals unknown to each other.[11] Mikhailovsky's views, predicated as they were upon a binary concept of human personality, need not have been very clear, or true, or even very relevant to art. Yet they exercised a strong and lasting influence on Tolstoy's critics and helped produce the image of a writer full of contradictions and paradoxes, always at war with himself.

War and Peace is in many of its aspects an emphatically earthy novel. This led some Russian symbolist critics, among them Dmitry Merezhkovsky (1866–1941), a prominent writer and philosopher, to perceive in Tolstoy's works a lack of opposition between man and nature, a situation whose consequences lie in the moral realm, for if nature is by definition amoral, then the world of Tolstoy's heroes might be amoral as well.[12] The question then is: How does one assess and receive art in which morality is an irrelevance? Merezhkovsky sought an answer in a comparison between Tolstoy and Dostoyevski, noting that in Dostoyevski we first learn to know a person's inner life, the soul, and in light of this knowledge the body becomes important not of itself, but as a symbol, or, as it were, an icon of the spirit. Tolstoy, on the other hand, goes from the physical to the spiritual, so that in the end a person's inner life becomes a sort of metaphor for the life of the flesh, and by extension, for all that is organic life in nature. Dostoyevski, accordingly, is a "seer of the spirit," while Tolstoy is a "seer of the flesh." From this distinction, Merezhkovsky develops an image of the moral dimension in Tolstoy: "Yes, there exists some sort of irrepressible religious idea in humanity, an idea from time beyond mind, and still not thought through to the end, that returns again and again, not only about fleshless holiness, but also about *sacred flesh*, about the transition from the human to the divine not only through things of the spirit but also through animal nature."[13]

Merezhkovsky may be right, but *War and Peace* in its image of life is a novel tremendously rich in endless variations of transition not through the flesh to the divine, but rather to a state of being where the spirit becomes symbolic of the flesh, and the subtle movements of the soul point to the reality of stones and grass. For instance, in Prince Andrey's slow descent into oblivion, what is happening to him becomes more and more important to us, because our own comprehension of life and death increases steadily as we watch how his body degenerates. The contemporary critic John Bayley makes a similar point when he notes that Pierre Bezukhov seems to "lack body" in the scene of execution of supposed Moscow incendiaries by the French.[14] The reason for this, according to Bayley, is that the intensity of the moment and its universality as both human experience and metaphysical event do not permit our perceptions of Pierre to be limited by his bodily reality. Nevertheless, it is true that most spiritual experiences in the novel *are* thus limited by the flesh. Bayley further notes that as Tolstoy perceives everything through and as a mode of his own self, he tends to simplify the world, including the dichotomy between body and flesh, to his own dimensions. "Tolstoy," says Bayley, "can juggle with the flesh as with truth and reason, forcing it to conform to the same kind of willed simplicity" (Bayley, 74).

A new stage in Tolstoy criticism opened up with the arrival of Soviet power in Russia. The Soviet establishment, much concerned with its cultural legitimacy, claimed the major literary classics as pathfinders for the revolution. Some works, like those of Dostoyevski, could not be reprocessed for a long time because of a lack of proper conceptual formula for their sovietization. The process was somewhat easier with Tolstoy, because Lenin had provided such a formula in his essays on Tolstoy, written between 1908 and 1911. There he set up a binary opposition between Tolstoy "the mirror of the revolution" who mercilessly tore down all the pretenses of bourgeois society and Tolstoy the conservative, patriarchal peasant autocrat obsessed by "one of the most odious things on earth, namely, religion."[15] This political reading became the main line of Soviet criticism of Tolstoy throughout the Stalin years and beyond.

The Russian formalists, a group of critics that flourished from about 1916 to the mid-1930s,[16] brought a more technical approach, reading the literary text as a special, artistic language with its own autonomous synthesis of form and meaning. Viktor Shklovsky (b. 1893) undertook the study of *War and Peace* in terms of tension between the traditional requirements of the novelistic genre and the need to defend the landowning class against attacks by the radical critics.[17] In the end, according to Shklovsky, Tolstoy deformed and expanded the novelistic genre at the same time as he "canonized the legend" of the Russian aristocracy that fought Napoleon. Beyond these points, however, the unity of *War and Peace* is a unity of developing perception of the artistic process itself in the minds of both the author and the reader. This perception creates the idea of the continuum of life as an aesthetic experience, depicted in the novel as an ongoing stream, shaping the lives of its characters and our image of the course of history, as well as our notion of the genre and dimensions of the work.[18]

Another lasting contribution by Shklovsky was the idea of "making strange," or "de-automation," as it applied to Tolstoy's work in general and to *War and Peace* in particular. Regarded through the prism of conventions, things lose their unique identity[19] and become mere automatic signals. Estrangement from convention enables us to look at things without a priori assumptions, as if for the first time.[20] Tolstoy frequently used this device to produce a striking new impression on the reader. Thus, in Book 8 of *War and Peace*, Natasha sees an opera performance without understanding anything, as a sort of grotesque ritual, and the resulting shocking effect "debunks" all our ideas about opera as a form of art.[21]

Among the formalists, Boris Eikhenbaum has produced the most thoroughgoing background research of the history of Tolstoy's ideas for *War and Peace*. He was motivated by two basic propositions: 1) that one must approach Tolstoy not "with bare hands," but with the knowledge of factors contemporary to the writing of the novel, and which create a resonance for the text, and 2) that there was an evolution of Tolstoy's intentions, from a mere desire to give vignettes of Russian landowning family life, to the goal of a historical novel that then would be an epic panorama of personal and historical events.[22] Eikhenbaum mentions several French, German, and Russian historians and social thinkers whose ideas on war, historical figures, and the philosophy of history clearly parallel Tolstoy's own.[23] He also notes that both Slavophilism and Westernism were for Tolstoy categories of the moral and not the intellectual order: what they represented were various modes of behavior and attitudes toward life emerging from personal perceptions. Certainly, the novel's ideas derive their ultimate shape from constant interaction between the characters' perceptions and the authorial voice.

Leaving aside the framework of Lenin's model or the formalists' contributions, Soviet commentary on *War and Peace* in general tended to focus on the question of genre. Gradually, the Soviet critics elevated the novel to the plane of the epic. Because epics in general tend to describe any culture in its historical depth and bring out a nation's lasting features, then *War and Peace* could be read almost as Russia's own grandiose statement about itself, one that sums up its essence across all time. Eventually, there emerged a genre designation commensurate with such greatness. The novel was to be called "novel-epos" (*roman-èpopoeia*).[24] This term has been accepted by most scholars, except for a few, such as E. Kupreyanova, who noted quite reasonably that the term *novel-epos* is in essence not scholarly but rhetorical.[25]

Scholarly analysis continued in the service of rhetoric as Tolstoy was being praised for his "realism" (a term that in the Soviet Union had a political rather than literary meaning)—that is, for his patriotism and love of the common Russian people because of their heroic qualities. Notwithstanding this political discourse, there were, of course, quite a few meticulous scholars who contributed a great deal to genuine literary study of the novel, among them, E. Zaidenshnur, V. F. Asmus, L. D. Opul'skaya, S. Bocharov, and others.

In the West, Tolstoy's friend and translator Aylmer Maude thought that *War and Peace*, although a family novel, accomplished "what had previously been done by the epic." It did so because Tolstoy had developed "a technique of analysis by which he could lay his finger on the mechanism of the internal preparation of human action" (Maude, 417). This allowed the author to go to the deep layers of consciousness where, presumably, one could feel life's epic stream. Percy Lubbock, on the other hand, complained that there was no center to the novel, because Tolstoy did not know how to blend together his two themes, war and peace. Henry James thought that *War and Peace* had practically no esthetic structure at all, and was instead a "loose baggy monster." Even Tolstoy himself seemed to him like "a monster harnessed to his great subject—all human life!"[26]

Images of Tolstoy softened considerably in the views of later critics. In fact, many thought that *War and Peace* was a quite conventional nineteenth-century novel, one not much different from European novels of the time. One critic, Donald Davie, even said that "there was perhaps never an artist of such power who was so little of an innovator as Tolstoy."[27]

R. F. Christian, another critic who believes *War and Peace* to be in the main a regular novel, ascribes to it a moral purpose approaching the Victorian ideal, even though "Tolstoy has an unfortunate tendency from time to time to call the virtues he admires specifically Russian": "Broadly speaking it is the contrast between two opposite states: on the one hand selfishness, self-indulgence, self-importance, and the attendant evils of careerism, nepotism, vanity, affectation and the pursuit of purely private pleasures; on the other hand a turning outwards from the self, a groping towards something bigger, an endeavour to surmount individualism, a recognition that the cult of the self is an unworthy alternative to the service of one's neighbours, one's family, the community and the country at large" (Christian, 105).

The Tolstoy and Dostoyevski specialist Edward Wasiolek disagrees completely on this point: "Despite a tradition of critical opinion that has insisted on formulating Tolstoy's value center in a conventional Christian and humanistic manner, Tolstoy seems to be saying the very opposite. He seems to be saying that life beats full *when one lives for oneself*, and beats less full *when one lives for others*."[28] In Wasiolek's discussion, this issue of "living for oneself" directly leads to some basic questions concerning the structure and the philosophical nature of the novel. At the outset, Wasiolek notes Isaiah Berlin's concern that at the base of the novel there should lie some common truth "toward which the 'good' characters tend and *from* which the unsympathetic characters have departed" (Wasiolek 65). This truth must affect the style, structure, and all the artistic devices of the novel, and it must be visible, perceived at any point, and in every detail of the text. In relation to this notion of truth borrowed from Berlin, Wasiolek also comes up with a structural scheme in regard to the characters in the novel:

> If one were to use an image to explain the deflection of life from the truth, it would consist of a center with concentric circles of increasing size and distance from the center. The distance of each concentric circle from the center would be the measure of deflection from the truth. Some characters like Prince Vassily Boris, Julie, and Ellen would be condemned to some outer circle, there to revolve without change and life throughout the novel. Others, like Nikolay and Princess Marya, would revolve in nearer circles without change until a decisive moment in their lives propelled them for a time into the inner core. Pierre would stumble in and out of it. Natasha, for a while, and Platon Karataev would stand in the very center. (Wasiolek, 70)

Ultimately, this truth can be articulated upon observation of Tolstoy's epilogues, where the central question is the dichotomy between free will and determinism. Noting that in the novel those characters seem the freest who are most concretely immersed in being themselves, that is, those that respond to the force of reality around them with the greatest intensity, Wasiolek proposes in Tolstoy a different concept of freedom from any that would require freedom to mean free choice of action:

> True freedom then is for Tolstoy not the power to initiate events abstractly, as if one were exempt from space and time and from preceding conditions, but the consciousness of reality. The fuller and richer the consciousness (*soznanie*), the freer one is. Such a conception of freedom will appear strong only if one judges it from what is for Tolstoy the unreal conception of freedom as the

24

initiation of events. Natasha is "free" at the ball because she experiences concretely and immediately what is going on inside and outside her, not because she makes some 'free' choice. Her freedom is the richness and plenitude of consciousness, that is, the immediate experience of much reality. (Wasiolek, 125)

The full possession of one's consciousness also seems to John Bayley a characteristic of Tolstoy's art. Bayley translates the idea of consciousness into the notion of conviction that one is automatically always right in perceiving that he or she exists and that what he or she perceives is true, and spoke of Tolstoy's "massive and casual assumption that the world is as he sees it, and as he says it is" (Bayley, 58). Accordingly, Tolstoy in *War and Peace* strives to make life "simple and clear" in the manner of mere biological manifestations, and this simplicity gives the novel the character of being a sort of Homeric narrative full of the rightness (as opposed to righteousness) of its being itself.[29] Nonetheless, Tolstoy did not think the world was a literary rhetorical device. The prescriptive conventions in art cannot prevail in a confrontation with what Tolstoy so confidently took to be reality. As were other critics, Philip Rahv was overwhelmed by the impression of simplicity produced by Tolstoy's infinitely complex work: "The art of Tolstoy is of such irresistible simplicity and truth, is at once so intense and so transparent in all of its effects, that the need is seldom felt to analyze the means by which it becomes what it is, that is to say, its method or sum of techniques. In the bracing Tolstoyan air, the critic, however addicted to analysis, cannot help doubting his own task. . . ."[30]

This reverent surrender of the critic's functions before the impenetrable simplicity of Tolstoy's work is rather different from the willingness of earlier readers to find fault with the novel because it was so difficult to approach. In describing *War and Peace* as either a novel, an epic, or an *epopoeia*, some critics impose upon it a particular grid of their own expectations. To the degree that the text resists such impositions, it does appear to be poorly organized, James's "baggy monster." Recently, Gary Saul Morson took another approach. He proposed that things that seem like irregularities and imperfections might actually be evidence of some new structural principle.

Morson calls this principle "narration by potential" and explains it thus: "An author who follows this method, or persuades others that he follows it, does not know at the outset what the work will turn out to be when complete. Rather, beginning with only a loose set of principles and resources, the author allows the work to 'shape itself' as it is being written. With no conclusion in mind, he deliberately cultivates the unexpected; structure is what it turns out to be, connections emerge without premeditation, and unity becomes only a unity of process. Integrity is ex post facto" (Morson, 182). According to such a method, "all events are the products both of chance and of complex and multiple causal lines." Such a reading accords well with Tolstoy's idea that it is not possible to plan ahead any complex events, such as a battle, and that there is no way to determine historical causality, except again by imposing one's own schemes upon time past. Morson also perceives what might be called a "principle of waste" in the novel: "We watch incidents that may or may not contribute to the plot; we see some come to nothing, others contribute to a greater or lesser degree; and we see, after a great deal of reading, an overall design in which plots emerge and fail to emerge from a mass of events that could, we feel, sustain many other plots" (Morson, 150).

Tolstoy's text thus seems to resemble nature itself. In both, there is tremendous waste: Seeds do or do not take hold at random, and there is no way to predict every breath of wind that may bring young plants to the soil's surface.

Nevertheless, we cannot escape the knowledge that the novel is something made by a human author and that therefore it has imposed a particular structure upon depicted reality; consequently, we will only gain the full benefits of the work if we continue to apply our critical and imaginative faculties to it.

A READING

4

Conception and Growth of the Novel

In a way, the story told in *War and Peace* began with children. In 1863, while teaching the peasant boys on his estate in Yasnaya Polyana, Tolstoy decided to give them some lessons in history. The pupils did not respond well to the remote ancient deeds of Hebrews or Persians because these had nothing to do with the children's lives and their own country. When Tolstoy turned to Russia, however, and particularly to its Napoleonic Wars, everyone became excited and took a lively interest, personalizing and commenting on the distant events, so that a peculiar world was created, peopled simultaneously by children of that day and by the heroes of yesteryear. Transported to that time in their imagination, the children became the equivalents of Andrey, Pierre, Natasha, and the others we read about in the novel itself. As to the treatment of history, Tolstoy readily admitted that what he told the children was not really history, but rather a fairy tale that aroused in them a national, patriotic feeling. The effect, therefore, was like that of a work of art: Cold facts became personally meaningful when suffused and transformed by emotion, and a reality grew out of personal perceptions.[1] To this extent, the history lessons of Yasnaya Polyana could be seen as an early prototype of the novel.

A number of critics have noted that Tolstoy's happy, early married life on the peaceful estate of Yasnaya Polyana combined with his war experiences to create a fertile ground in his mind from which *War and Peace* could be shaped. There are also points of contact with Tolstoy's earlier fiction. In Tolstoy, as in so many other authors, any given text is really but a link in a continuing inner discourse spanning his entire creative life, so that identifiable factors in a particular work must be correlated with a flood of others not necessarily considered before. From Tolstoy's trilogy *Childhood* (1852), *Adolescence* (1854), and *Youth* (1857) came the art of minute reproduction of reality as experience suffused with imagination. In this early trilogy Tolstoy also learned how to imply larger ideas in very small fragments of reality and how to observe a microcosm and make it into a world, as in *Childhood*, when the busy world of ants was observed by young Irten'ev.[2] By this time he had already mastered the highly intense and intimate reality of domestic scenes. In them, each nuance can precipitate an entire flood of emotions, which, in turn, organize enclosed spaces into special microcosms, little worlds shared only by members of a select community, such as family and close friends.[3]

These techniques are seen in *War and Peace* developed to the fullest extent. The *Sevastopol' Sketches* (1855) and the early stories of military life in the Caucasus lay the foundations for Tolstoy's portrayal of war as an individual human experience. As in *War and Peace*, there is a series of concrete and detailed perceptions, each comprising a single individual's entire universe, that intertwine and blend with the perceptions of every other individual. The result is an entirety, like the flow of a river, perceived by the reader as something that is continuously happening in his or her own mind. In *War and Peace* it may be just this perception that makes us feel as though we are dealing with an epic. The *Sevastopol' Sketches* were also extremely important because there Tolstoy opened up and exposed all the infinitely complex processes that go on in the mind of someone in the shadow of death. Outside that person's consciousness, however, the inhuman mass slaughter, an abomination perpetrated against the background of verdant, blossoming nature, was shown to be a part of that nature as well, one of its processes, just as we see it in *War and Peace*.[4]

Also, some characters from *War and Peace*, such as the restless seeker Pierre Bezukhov and the socially alienated young officer Andrey Bolkonsky, can be seen in the prototype of Olenin, the self-absorbed protagonist of *The Cossacks* (1863). Likewise, the animal vitality of Maryanka, the Cossack girl in the story, extends across time and social status to the irrepressible Natasha Rostova.

At first, the novel was to be called "The Decembrists," after the group of intellectuals and army officers who came back from Paris after Napoleon's final defeat and brought with them liberal, even revolutionary ideas about constitutional monarchy and fundamental human rights, and led a failed uprising against the tsar in December 1825. Originally, Tolstoy chose a point in his present, 1856, and began the story with the return from Siberian exile of the aging Decembrist Pierre Bezukhov and his wife Natasha from Siberian exile. This beginning turned out to be a false start because Tolstoy could not reconcile the idea of Pierre as someone who suddenly entered the text as a complete character with the notion of Pierre's past being unknown. For Tolstoy life was an unbroken process, not a set of stationary frames, and he could not understand even his own imaginary heroes without imagining a past for them that would illuminate the present.[5] Thus, Tolstoy explained: "I moved from the present time to the year 1825, a period of error and unhappiness for my hero, and I abandoned what I had begun. But even in the year 1825 my hero was already a grown-up family man. In order to understand him, I had to move once again, back to his youth, and his youth coincided with the period of 1812, so glorious for Russia" (*W&P*, 1364).

Yet, for a writer who thinks in terms of constant movement, 1812 could not serve as a stable starting point either. Even if the young Pierre became understandable, Tolstoy could not assess the true spirit of his time without going back to the previous period of Russia's defeats in 1805.[6] It is also very important to note here that the novel was being written against the background of Russia's defeat in the Crimean War, a loss that weighed so heavily on people's minds for decades that it called for a different story, one in which Russia could be shown triumphant. Thus, according to Tolstoy, a chain was to be created "from that time onward through the historical events of 1805, 1807, 1812, 1825 and 1856" (*W&P*, 1364).

Actually, Tolstoy managed to walk only halfway across this bridge of time from 1805 to 1856, because his burden of needing to describe the constant changes in all aspects of the novel grew heavier. According to Boris Eikhenbaum, one should distinguish at least four periods in Tolstoy's work on the novel: 1) work done in 1863, after discontinuing "The Decembrists"; 2) work in 1864; 3) work in 1865–66 under the title "All's Well That Ends Well"; and 4) work from 1867–69, under the title *War and Peace* (Eikhenbaum II, 244).

The first 38 chapters, constituting the first part of the finished novel, were published serially in 1865 in the *Russian Messenger* under the title *1805*. The next installment, called *War*, appeared in the *Messenger* in 1866, and in June 1866 these two parts came out in book form with the title *1805*. Soon afterwards, in negotiations with a printer who agreed to publish the work as a whole, Tolstoy crossed out that title and inserted *War and Peace* instead.

Changes in the book's title seem of themselves to indicate Tolstoy's growing recognition of the expanding scope and universality of the work taking shape under his pen. "The Decembrists" restricts the field of vision to the affairs of a small, failed group, indeed, mainly to just one person—Pierre. "All's Well That Ends Well" recalls the Shakespearean comedy; at the very least, it points to a narrow, private scope of concerns and events focused upon family affairs, almost like a comedy of manners. On the other hand, "1805" extends the arena to a historical scale of events, but the novel does not reach its epic space and philosophical universality until it is conceived in the all-embracing terms that are implicit in its final title, "War and Peace."

The structure of the text itself began to emerge slowly from the broken shapes of many visions and revisions, and in confrontation with the standard norms of a "regular" novel. In the end, we have a structure that straddles three paths that a novel may take. One path tells the story of a number of private lives in several families of Russian aristocrats living in an epoch-making time. The other leads to a conventional historical novel in which fictional characters play relatively minimal supporting roles to historical personages and events. The third path creates a *roman à thèse* in which events and characters unfold on both public and private planes, and are depicted in both fictional and historical modes that serve as devices for developing a universal thought, such as, in *War and Peace*, a philosophy of history that emerges from the framework of all-encompassing questions about free will and human destiny.

Most traditional Russian prose actually does choose one or another of these and similar approaches as their governing methodological principle. Tolstoy, however, is unique in that he developed all three alternatives, each to the degree needed for him to coordinate an overall structure unique to his own work and to any Russian prose of his time. He set the action across long distances—from Moscow to Austria—and over a sufficient time span—from 1805 to 1812, and a few years beyond—in order to give himself a sufficient continuum of fictional time and space to allow for the development of events and the ideas they engender.

On the fictional plane, *War and Peace* is the story of several aristocratic Russian families engaged in their private affairs, but also caught up in the huge historical events that intrude on their lives, changing them radically. Most of the fictional narrative space is taken by the Rostovs, a typical Russian landowning family of the time. Old Count Ilya Rostov is kindly, foolish in the affairs of the world, and therefore forever in debt. He has a quietly selfish wife, Natalya, an unpleasant daughter, Vera, a helpless ward, Sonya, and an irrepressible, wonderful youngest daughter, Natasha, who will gradually take center stage as a symbol of Russia's strength and joy of life in the face of catastrophic adversity. An older son, Nikolay, becomes a hussar and rides off to fight Napoleon, and his younger brother, Petya, a mere boy, is killed in one of the last Russian ambushes on the retreating French troops. Nikolay Rostov alternates between the front, where he learns about the terror and strange beauty of war, and home, where he dances, hunts wild game in the company of the entire Rostov brood, and pursues a desultory romance with the ward, Sonya, until his mother stops him. When he does get married, it is to Princess Mary, daughter of the retired, wrinkled, desiccated, and proudly eccentric Prince Nikolay Bolkonsky, a former general in the service of Catherine the Great. Bolkonsky's is the second important family in the novel; his clan is linked with the Rostovs not only because of Nikolay's eventual marriage to Mary, but also because of a love affair that could have but did not end up in the marriage of the general's son, Andrey, to Natasha Rostova. This potentially neat, symmetrical arrangement of family connections and destinies is disrupted first by the war and second by Natasha's frustration with her solitude while waiting at Otradnoe, the Rostovs' estate, for Andrey, which leads her into an unfortunate flirtation with Anatoly Kuragin. The Kuragins are the third important family. There is the old Prince Vassily, a courtier, schemer, and fool, his daughter, Helen (Hélène), a stunningly beautiful and stately smiling idiot, and her brother, Hyppolite, who is exactly like Helen in every detail, except that he is ugly. Finally, there is Anatoly, the empty-headed, handsome rake who almost destroys Natasha's whole life. The entire family cannot distinguish right from wrong, nor do they possess any other moral beliefs; Tolstoy himself refers to them at one point as a "brood of vipers."

Hundreds of other characters swarm around these three families, and viewed together they constitute the living body of the Russian nation that is so gravely violated and wounded by the thrust of Napoleon's attack. The attack itself, and the entire general course of the war, represent the plot's historical dimension. It is interesting to note, moreover, that actual historical personages are few and, except for the field marshal Kutuzov, exist on their own abstract plane, as if they were gods of history, remote from the living and dying humanity around them. In that sense, one might say that in the novel the reality of history as a set of events, on the level of dirt and sweat, blood and death, agony and rejoicing, is carried on by fictional people; the author's imagination is more real than the actual processes of history. By this method of writing, Tolstoy strengthens his argument that even outside the sphere of fiction, historical or not, history's forces reside in the movements of the masses themselves and not in their remote leaders. He also constructs the image of reality not as a set of facts conveyed by a narrator, but as a stream of experiences and perceptions lived by the fictional characters.

Since the portrayal of events, their backgrounds, and human experiences are so very closely tied to the expository statements at the end of the novel, one may say that this unity is also Tolstoy's unique achievement. What he did was obliterate the dividing line between narration and argument and thus also between artistic and expository language. There are a lot of very intense and sometimes abstract arguments about humankind, God, sin, and salvation in the works of Dostoyevski, but they are carried on by the characters themselves, in the course of their dialogues with each other, which, in turn, promote the line of conflict and action. In Tolstoy this vehicle is used minimally, and when it is employed, as in Andrey's last conversation with Pierre, just before the Battle of Borodino, during which they discussed the dreadful meaninglessness of war, it does not have the structure of an argument, but rather that of an outburst of emotion. At their extremes, narrated action and articulated argument are easily distinguishable from each other, but the zone where they meet is not clearly recognizable in the novel. We might add that the novel's entire ambience, perhaps its essence, resides precisely in that uncertain zone.

In the view of many critics, Tolstoy's approach made it necessary to break down a number of conventions once considered obligatory for a "well-written" novel. Viktor Shklovsky, a perceptive reader, notes that novelistic conventions kept requiring representations of characters and actions that had little or nothing to do with the inner sense of truth that Tolstoy was struggling to articulate. Struggling against these conventions, he kept building new models in his mind, hoping to perceive the complete and truthful model of life he knew he possessed (Shklovsky 1963, 399ff.). In reading Tolstoy, it is very important that we understand this presumed ultimate model itself, not as a fully realized stationary shape, but as a dynamic, developing entity, a process that enters from Tolstoy's mind into our own, constantly restructuring the entire edifice of our own norms, assumptions, prejudices, and perceptions.

Many critics were interested in the direction of such restructuring. Was the novel first intended to be a family chronicle with elements of military life expanded to broad historical dimensions in the process of its creation, or was it meant from the beginning to be a grand historical-fictional epic, something reminiscent of *The Iliad*? Boris Eikhenbaum and R. F. Christian argue the two sides of the question. Eikhenbaum holds to the premise that for Tolstoy the important events took place inside a person, in the ambiance of family life, among ordinary things, and in that sense the novel was to be a history of family life and mores against a muted background of large events. Nonetheless, many readers saw that the domestic ambiance described was, in its various details and incidents of family life, a reflection of Tolstoy's own home in the 1860s, and not of the epic drama of 1812. Even the intellectual issues pertaining to legislative reforms and other matters, though they represented the events and trends of the beginning of the century, were depicted in the spirit of Tolstoy's own time frame. Only later, in part influenced by his friends Strakhov and S. S. Urusov,[7] did Tolstoy begin to feel that his novel would not amount to much if historical questions were not given much more prominence. That decision changed the very tone of the novel, giving it a more philosophical bent and a higher style. These changes in the conception of the novel made it somewhat uneven both in language and in the choice and depiction of events, especially since, as Eikhenbaum points out, the first publication in installments "made it impossible for Tolstoy to rework the early parts to conform with the changes in the later ones" (Eikhenbaum II, 386). On the other side of the argument, R. F. Christian, while agreeing that the early draft begins with family life, nevertheless thinks that all the elements that make up *War and Peace* were there from the very beginning in one form or another, "and make nonsense of the suggestion that they—or some of them—were necessitated by a later elevation of genre" (Christian, 212).

Whichever point of view we choose, we can still see the novel growing and rising in our mind's eye like some giant organism that was born, so to speak, in the grass, down among the simplest family events where all things must start. We can see how it spreads upward and outward like a tree, drawing in and feeding upon more and more realistic aspects: objects, time, space, human thoughts and the edifice of ideas that comprise civilization, terrible and beautiful human feelings from which arise the atrocity of war and the infinity of life, and finally, the indifference of death. Just this last notion alone, that Tolstoy's novel would draw nourishment for all its vitality from the ultimate indifference of death, may seem too terrible and far-fetched to contemplate. Yet the death of Andrey Bolkonsky, becoming from our present point of view the focal point of the novel, exudes, as the Buddhists might say, a certain peace that passeth understanding; Tolstoy himself said in his old age that "death is the greatest good."[8] From this perspective, all human stirrings, their war and their peace, might appear small indeed, and we begin to grasp the fatally wounded Andrey's perception at Austerlitz, that gray skies alone seem important at that timeless moment.

But we might also think of life not as something an author is writing about, but as something that grows simultaneously in our minds and in the text as we read it. How many dimensions, for instance, can there be to Natasha? As *War and Peace* expands in our minds, we may begin to see that this question can be answered only in terms of the constantly accumulating new contexts in which she lives and acts. These contexts, in turn, bring with them wide-ranging issues, all of which contribute to Natasha's image and function in the novel, an argument we shall return to later. The same case can be made for Pierre, and Nikolay Rostov, and all the other characters. Thus the novel becomes something other than a mere aggregate of ideas that happened to cross Tolstoy's field of vision as he went on writing over the years, but instead truly evolves into an organism, all of whose parts came to be as a consequence of some algorithm, a genetic code of sorts, that was there in Tolstoy's mind as he approached his subject. One might say that there are overall patterns in the novel that emerge from a particular central feeling of the author's, and that these patterns present an effort by Tolstoy to articulate that feeling.

One potential algorithm may be the organic principle: The novel can be regarded as an organism that has embedded in each of its detailed substructures the whole DNA code, as if it were a body cell. The expansion of the novel, its realization of an increasing number of dimensions, might then seem to tell another story besides its own— that of the artist's growing authority and control over this endless and incomprehensible realm we call reality, to the point where he can and does create a towering work of art. Modern criticism has been developing this understanding as an effective tool for exploring the nonconformity and originality of the novel. Morson, in accordance with his view that the novel is structured to illustrate the lack of formal causal structures in actual life, calls this method "parodic": "Tolstoy argues that all received narrative forms contain implicit assumptions about the way events happen, and that these assumptions are false. Because they are usually implicit, the assumptions are rarely subject to scrutiny. But *War and Peace* does subject them to scrutiny, and Tolstoy uses a variety of arguments and aesthetic strategies to demonstrate the inadequacy of existing models and genres. Thus the work is deeply parodic: it satirizes all historical writing, and all novels" (Morson, 83).

Nevertheless, the dichotomy of the basic conception of the work remains and is present on two levels. One is related to issues of literary genre; many readers still ask the question: Is the novel a set of stories of family life, or is it a heroic epic of the legend that is Russia? The other level pertains to the basic conception of the process of narration: Is it an idea that flows along without premeditation, one indifferent to the particular means or situations by which it shall embody itself, or is it a fixed idea, one that submits all events, incidental or not, to its structuring design? Stated in such terms, this dichotomy regarding the very conception of the novel echoes the opposition between freedom and necessity that we find in the structure of Tolstoy's expository argument: Either life is governed by understandable laws according to which we can plot the basic map of history, or the causes and consequences of events are so innumerable and untraceable that all we can do is respond to the impulses of the moment. One could perhaps think of these dichotomies, or contradictions, in themselves as defining the basic conception of the novel. War and peace, fiction and history, rational order and organic growth, honor and corruption, the individual and the people, the idyll and the epic, death and life, love and filth—the work seems to be held together by the very tension of these contradictions. Is there a resolution that would become, by the same token, the key to the novel?

Perhaps the nature of this mysterious key can be found upon closer observation of how the novel works, an activity we shall now undertake.

5

The World of Perceptions

It has been said that in the stories of Anton Chekhov the nature of reality is fluid and relative to the observer.[1] As much could be said of Lev Tolstoy's work.[2] In reading *War and Peace* we engage in not one, but three different worlds. One is a world seen by someone resembling Tolstoy himself, and it consists of general commentaries and historical-philosophical arguments pertaining to the events and circumstances described. This alter ego of Tolstoy's stands on intermediate ground somewhere between the text of the novel and Tolstoy's own mind. In places where the narration of plot is interrupted to make observations that are not part of the fictional flow, this narrator almost completely blends with Lev Tolstoy, becoming a writer who contemplates the general implications of the tale he is telling to the issues of history.

The second world is a hybrid creation in which the author-narrator's attitudes and convictions are presented to us as if they were the thoughts and experiences of the characters themselves. This narrative space becomes especially important when the personal life of a character is confronted directly with the processes of history. For instance, in Book 9 (according to Maude's arrangement) we see the generals at the war council in Drissa discussing how to confront Napoleon's invasion;

the action seems like meaningless posturing as we watch the scene through the eyes of Prince Andrey, who thinks Tolstoy's thoughts as if they were his own. Similarly, in Book 11, the little peasant girl Malasha overhears the war council in Fili, after the Battle of Borodino, and knows that in the general discussion "granddad" Kutuzov is right and "long-coat" (General Bennigsen) wrong. Malasha's perceptions, simple and childish as they are, seem profound in the light of Tolstoy's expository comments directly preceding this scene, because there he insists that Kutuzov took the right course of action by withdrawing from Moscow. The same device is used in other critical junctures in the characters' lives. When Natasha loses her power to resist the temptations of Anatoly Kuragin (Book 8), she is at the opera in a distraught state, and all that is happening on the stage seems absolutely meaningless to her. This young woman's fleeting impression, however, is thoroughly confirmed by Tolstoy in a later text, "What Is Art?" (1897), as his own opinion on the absurdity of modern drama, and it is clear from that essay that he held this opinion of conventional art throughout his life.

In the third world the character is truly "at home," inside a space generated by his own perceptions and in which both the narrator and the reader are outsiders. This realm is a circumscribed world reflected in the minds of fictional characters through the prism of their personal feelings in such a way that they perceive their lives to reflect a universal mirror image.[3] In intimate settings where each detail is thoroughly familiar to a given character, it seems as if the entire world is contained in this little pocket of personal reality, and conversely, this unique and intimate space in a sense *becomes* that person. In this way, objects and circumstances may acquire a "soul"; they can be "possessed" by a person's inner world and this world itself may be "possessed" by something that seems to enter it from the outside. In *War and Peace*, this is how individual feelings acquire a material substance that establishes a personal identity, which we can also call one's voice, or discourse. When placed in various relationships with other voices, these intimate worlds of personal feelings become the component parts of a complex ongoing dialogue, or conversation, or perhaps even symposium, which weaves and binds the organic strands of the edifice of the novel.

A self-defined universe of perceptions naturally tends toward the hermetical; hence, the issue of communication becomes very important. In a sense, it could be the most important issue in the entire work, in conjunction with the dynamics, the organic functioning of the text as a whole, and the philosophical question about existential human solitude under the roof of the universe, an idea implicit in the novel.

One aspect of this question that is very important in *War and Peace*, is communication between nature and humans. From the very beginning Tolstoy was opposed to the sentimentalist approach of ascribing human feelings to things in nature, as he states in his diary in 1851: "Others say that *mountains, it seemed, were saying something* and *the leaves something else again* and that *the trees were calling somewhere*. How can such thoughts occur? You have to work at it to stuff your head with such nonsense" (*PSS*, vol. 46, 65).

When speaking in the narrator's voice, Tolstoy always tried to avoid such illusions, but he also understood that things in nature must be granted an integrity of their own, as if they too could be aware of their surroundings and send out messages. The only way to portray things in this manner and also avoid the sentimentalists' pathetic fallacy was to show how his characters felt as they were walking through a world in which all things spoke to them in their own special language.

In this way, Tolstoy resolved his early frustration at being unable to depict reality so that it would indeed be "real," and not mere ink marks on a piece of paper, as he said in 1851:

> I was relaxing behind the camp a minute ago. A marvelous night! The moon had just come up from behind the hill and shed its light on two small, thin, low clouds; a cricket behind me was singing his unceasing, melancholy tune; a frog was heard in the distance, and near the aul [a mountaineer village] dogs barked, tartars yelled; then again all would be quiet, and again all you heard was the chirping of the cricket, and the light, transparent cloud was floating past the close and the distant stars.
>
> I thought: let me go and describe what I saw. But how do you write this down? You have to sit behind an ink-stained table, take a gray piece of paper, ink; smear your fingers and write letters on the paper. The letters will make words, the words phrases, but

how can you transmit feeling? Isn't there some way to transfer to someone else the look in one's own eyes at the sight of nature? Description is not enough. (*PSS*, vol. 46, 65)

Tolstoy resolved this problem in his work by creating that "someone else" as a fictional character. Feeling could now be transmitted not by some miraculous way of making a magic evening out of a glob of ink, but by entering the minds of other, imaginary human beings and telling how they felt in their surroundings. The "look in one's own eyes" could then indeed be transferred to someone of Tolstoy's own creation. This effect does help the reader to respond to the author's effort to communicate, say, a magical evening, even though, of course, we are also watching the circular process of an author talking ultimately to himself.

What's important is that these created people could enter their imaginary worlds as if everything, being but reflections of themselves, belonged to the same order of existence—people, trees, rivers, sunlight—everything. Thus, most of what we see in *War and Peace*—landscapes, particular objects, faces, action—are reported by the narrator as the perceptions of the various characters themselves. Therefore, the world before us consists of a variety of different visions, each one being equally valid for every separate individual. Therefore, communication, the gravitational force that can keep this kaleidoscope of worlds together, is possible in the novel only to the extent that one person can understand and feel what is inside the horizons of another. Hence, that communication among separate individuals in the novel can take place only when a mutual empathy is present. It is this feeling of closeness to and identity with the novel's heroes, which occurs when the contents of our consciousness and knowledge coincide with those of the character, that has prompted some critics to complain that "Tolstoy knows everything," that is, he knows about his heroes as much as we feel we know about ourselves.

Such reciprocal feeling opens many channels of communication between protagonists, extending the functions of language beyond the verbal levels. Both verbal and nonverbal signals can communicate at once in several different codes: those of a word, a glance, a tone of voice, a particular movement, and so on. The actual relationships among people, the success of their communication, will be in part determined by how many "receivers" the other person has. The reader is also called upon here; Tolstoy appeals to the multiplicity in the reader's ability to respond. This ability will in turn be diminished or enhanced by the degree of our empathy with a character, that is, by our ability to become others while also remaining ourselves. In that sense, it might be said that Tolstoyan characters, or at least those endowed with intelligence and sensitivity, make their own being manifest not so much by sending verbal or action messages to the outside as by receiving them; existence is perception.

On the other hand, characters who lack the sensitivity and inner complexity to perceive messages are forever imposing themselves upon the world. Foremost among them in the novel is, of course, Napoleon, followed by a host of others, such as Dolokhov, Berg, Drubetskoy, and so on. When these characters do exchange perceptions, the process becomes a parody and a fake, representing all the amenities of polite society, all the rituals devised for reasons having little or nothing to do with real communication. In Tolstoy, all such artificial things represent what we are accustomed to calling "civilization."[4] A good example of this miscommunication appears on the very first page of *War and Peace*, where Prince Vassily is conversing at a ball with Madame Sherer, the hostess. They are exchanging remarks about politics and court life, and both are lying to each other without, as Tolstoy says, even wishing to be believed. Yet they understand each other well because they, too, share a mock "empathy" with each other, being attuned to the same code according to which their lies are actually figures of speech masking unpleasant truths about their relationship and life in general, truths that are better left unsaid. The most unpleasant among these truths is the obscure realization somewhere in their murky psyches that their lives are but meaningless posturings in front of the gaping eternal void. One might say without too much exaggeration that in such passages Tolstoy's idea of "worldly culture" seems like a function of the fear of death.

In such a semiotic universe, where things not only are but also signify, Tolstoy nevertheless avoids the danger of turning reality into a

Baudelairean "forest of symbols"[5]; things remain themselves, and the messages they carry arise not from some extraneous source, like a writer's style or beliefs, but from the core of their own being, that is, the messages seem like a particular mode in which things appear to exist. Landscapes, or indeed anything else in such a world, are not figurative, not literary tropes—they are real. Yet they do achieve the same effect as symbols and metaphors would. In *War and Peace* this effect is at work when things that are of themselves innocuous and that convey only a minimal meaning begin to communicate on many more levels when filtered through a character's perceptions. In contradistinction to Tolstoy's famous device of "making strange," in which things we thought we always knew well become suddenly alien, as if seen for the first time, here we see an opposite, mirrorlike device, "making familiar," in which indifferent, previously unnoticed objects suddenly seem to respond on the same wavelength as something personal and intimate inside of us.

One example of both devices working together is Nikolay's homecoming to Moscow, together with his friend Denisov, after the 1808 campaign. Denisov is a stranger to the family, and Tolstoy conveniently arranges for him to drink three bottles of wine and fall asleep as they approach the house, so that Denisov's own impressions of the house would not interfere with the delicate processes going on in Nikolay's mind. First of all, Nikolay feels that "the house stood cold and silent, as if quite regardless of who had come to it" (*W&P*, 320). The house has been "made strange"—it is not what Nikolay remembers. Note the fine shade of disappointment, rather like an accusation, that darkens Nikolays' heart, because in his mind his home had a duty to respond to him immediately, just as everyone in his family is expected to love him, for otherwise life would become totally incomprehensible, as it did at Schöngraben, where an excited Frenchman seemed intent on killing him "whom everybody loves." But the cold house did have a means of "making itself familiar" to Rostov. It was the door handle; it turned just as loosely as it always had before, a fact that used to make his mother angry. No one but Nikolay and his family knew about and, so to speak, interacted with this handle; this secret knowledge suddenly made the house familiar again and prepared Nikolay for the tumultuous welcome he received as soon as he went inside. Thus alienation and belonging, two large existential issues, depend on that single turn of the handle, on how Nikolay feels at that moment. And so, "Rostov reentered that world of home an childhood which has no meaning for anyone else" (*W&P*, 324). The point is that others might very well understand that there is a special meaning in that world, but the particular way of perceiving it is Rostov's alone. Tolstoy's ultimate aim is to stimulate the reader to break through his or her own aloneness and become a part of this special Rostov universe, thereby achieving that interactive level of communication with a character that the sentimentalists strove to achieve with nature.

A special euphoric space also envelops the Christmas episode, in Book 7, when Nikolai Rostov again comes home on leave. This time Tolstoy links his characters' perceptions with the idea of transformations, changing identities. As things change they begin to tell their own stories, in other words, they "become strange." Hence, the process of "making familiar" is started again and gives the episode a symbolic meaning pertaining to the young people's destinies while also establishing new modes of communication among them. The episode begins with Natasha, Nikolay, and Sonya sharing reminiscences from their early childhood, that "most distant place where dreams and realities blend" (*W&P*, 574). There is talk of metempsychosis, reincarnations in the form of animals or angels, and then the idea strikes them to become mummers, it being Yuletide. The young brother Petya is transformed into a Turkish girl, Nikolay becomes an old lady in a hoop skirt, and Natasha and Sonya, a hussar and a Circassian. The sleigh ride that follows, flickering rapidly and joyfully between "strange" and "familiar," further transforms everything into an utterly charming magic world: "'Where are we?' thought he [Nikolay]. 'Its the Kosoy meadow, I suppose. But no—this is something new I've never seen before. This isn't the Kosoy meadow nor the Dyomkin hill, and heaven only knows what it is! It is something new and enchanted'" (*W&P*, 579).

But there is something else. Sonya, the ward of the Rostov family, has been dreaming of marrying Nikolay some day. But she is somehow different from others. As reminiscences are being exchanged, she remains outside the magic circle: "What she recalled did not arouse the same poetic feeling as they experienced. She simply enjoyed their pleasure and tried to fit in with it" (*W&P*, 574). As Sonya changes into her mummer's costume, she seems exceptionally beautiful to everyone and herself feels "that now or never her fate would be decided" and that in her male attire "she seemed quite a different person" (*W&P*, 577). Then it is Nikolay's feelings that tell us what it means for her to be so different:

> Nicholas glanced round at Sonya, and bent down to see her face closer. Quite a new, sweet face with black eyebrows and mustaches peeped up at him from her sable furs—so close and yet so distant—in the moonlight.
> "That used to be Sonya," thought he, and looked at her closer and smiled.
> "What is it, Nicholas?"
> "Nothing," said he and turned again to the horses. (*W&P*, 578)

Sonya is not what she was. Sonya is distant. Nikolay tells her nothing about the many complex feelings inside him at this moment, many of which even he does not even know.[6] We realize in this instant that they will never get married, no matter what particular events in the future will separate them.

Natasha's feelings function as signs of her future, not only in happy scenes, but also in scenes designed to give the reader a feeling of impending disaster. One such scene describes Natasha at an opera performance. Here Tolstoy's basic device is, first, to use Natasha's perceptions as a means to "make strange" her surroundings at the opera house, and second, to make them evil. Natasha's doom is signified when she begins to "understand" and "appreciate" what she sees; soon after she finally succumbs to the lures of Anatoly Kuragin. In this way, Tolstoy insinuates his own convictions about the arts and mores of high society and also makes them a part of Natasha's destiny.

The episode is prepared for by Natasha's visit to the old Bolkonsky, Andrey's father, in her position as the prospective bride. Andrey is away, having followed his father's wish to postpone the marriage, Natasha is frustrated, distraught with her yearning for him, and Bolkonsky is angry that a girl he never met would take his son from him. During the visit he insults Natasha by appearing in his nightcap and sleeping gown and pretending not to know that she had come. The helpless Natasha also fails in her effort to make friends with Andrey's sister Marya, and leaves in a state of shock. That very evening, the Rostovs go to the opera.

In describing the opera (*W&P*, 620–26) Tolstoy inserts a series of markers that, when taken together, almost constitute another text, one that interprets the overall scene and encumbers it with implicit value judgments. In the audience there are ladies "with bare arms" and gentlemen in "brilliant uniforms," that is, there is nudity and vanity, two faces of the encroaching evil. Hundreds look at Natasha's "bare arms," which evoke a "crowd of memories, desires and emotions"—the temptation begins. Her delicate arm, "bare to the elbow," lays on the "velvet edge of the box," as if she were a naked woman in her sinful boudoir. Dolokhov and Anatoly Kuragin appear, extravagantly dressed, while Natasha looks with admiration at Julie Karagina's much-exposed "shoulders and pearls," and all the women "with gems on their bare flesh" look at the stage. There "one very fat girl in a white silk dress" sits on a bench, a man "with tight silk trousers" appears, and they start to sing. Natasha cannot listen to the music or follow the action; "she saw only the painted cardboard and the queerly dressed men and women," so pretentious and unnatural that she first was "ashamed" of them, and then "amused" by them (here is the danger signal: an emotional contact). Then Natasha's eyes stray to the "seminude women" in the tiers, including Hélène, Kuragin's sister, who, "apparently quite unclothed," sat with a tranquil smile. At this point, among the nakedness and the brilliant lights and the warmth of the crowd, Natasha begins to feel "intoxicated" and has "the strangest fancies," including "jumping off the edge of the box and singing in the air," an obvious sexual impulse.[7]

In the second act, there is a "hole in the canvas to represent the moon," and men are dragging away the fat maiden, singing loudly together with her, while Hélène turns to look at the Rostovs with "her whole bosom completely exposed." On the stage there are "men and women with bare legs," and the premiere danseuse, "with thick bare legs," dances with a man named Dupont, also "with bare legs," who receives "sixty thousand rubles a year" for this art. As the scene continues, Hélène is described as progressively more naked, her brother as ever more irresistible as he looks at her "with glittering eyes, smiling tenderly," and Natasha as more and more appreciative of the goings-on onstage. At the end of the episode, although Natasha knows that "nothing really happened," she nevertheless feels as though something dirty has entered her soul and created a barrier between her and her dream of Andrey. This is the beginning of her downfall, and with each progressive step some sort of moral filth, disguised as beauty, art, or the feminine charms of society, oozes onto the stage. Natasha's predicament reflects Tolstoy's thoughts as a narrator and author, and her feelings acquire the stain of corruption because of Tolstoy's negative bias toward glittering society. For us readers it begins to seem inevitable that Natasha is approaching the greatest trauma of her life.

One of the most moving episodes in the novel—young Petya Rostov's last night on earth (Book 12)—is drawn by Tolstoy on the infinitely fine line between Petya's perceptions of reality and his dreams, and, by metaphor, is extended to the dark, unknown realm between sleep and death. The episode is built on a binary principle, and the preliminary frame for it is laid out much earlier, in Book 7, during the famous episode of the wolf hunt at Otradnoe. During the posthunt celebration at the Rostov's uncle's house there is plain country food, the uncle plays his guitar, and Natasha expertly dances a folk dance without ever having been taught one. Young Petya sleeps right through all the clamor, with the music undoubtedly ringing in his ears.

As they all leave, Tolstoy gently touches an ominous note: The still-sleeping "Petya was carried out like a log and laid in the larger of the two traps" (W&P, 565). One cannot escape the visual suggestion of a dead soldier being brought out from the battlefield. So, we have a celebration of the indomitable Russian spirit, music, and an illusion of death. In Book 14 the situation is the reverse: We have death and an illusion of music. An enthusiastic tenderfoot volunteer, Petya was sent to join Denisov's forces, who are pursuing the retreating French as if they were the wolf hunted down in Book 7.[8] The French have Russian prisoners with them, including Pierre. Petya, still a child, has brought some raisins with which to treat the fierce Cossacks, and we recall a distant echo of the grand meal after the hunting party.[9] A counterpart of Petya is Vincent, a captured French drummer boy, whom the Cossacks nicknamed "Vesennij," a "boy of Springtime" (for in the forest there is a thaw); he will be killed at the end of the episode, together with the other French prisoners. He and Petya quickly become good friends. The night descends. Petya asks a Cossack to sharpen his saber, and sabre hissing against the whetstone produces a constant "ozheg-zheg" sound. Then, touched by the hand of slumber, the world is magically changed. Petya is "in a fairy kingdom, where nothing resembled reality. The big red blotch might really be the watchman's hut, or it might be a cavern leading to the very depths of earth. Perhaps the red spot was a fire, or it might be the eye of an enormous monster" (*W&P*, 1170). After this passage, Tolstoy employs an image that often carries the meaning of death in all literature:

> Perhaps he was really sitting on a wagon, but it might very well be that he was not sitting on a wagon but on a terribly high tower from which, if he fell, he would have to fall for a whole day or a whole month, or go on falling and never reaching the bottom.[10] . . . Ozheg-zheg, Ozheg-zheg . . . hissed the saber against the whetstone, and suddenly Petya heard an harmonious orchestra playing some unknown, sweetly solemn hymn. . . .
>
> "Oh, why—that was in a dream!" Petya said to himself, as he lurched forward. "It's in my ears. But perhaps it's music of my own. Well, go on, my music! Now!"
>
> He closed his eyes and, from all sides as if from a distance, sounds fluttered, grew into harmonies, separated, blended, and again all mingled into the same sweet and solemn hymn. "Oh, this is delightful! As much as I like and as I like!" said Petya to himself. He tried to conduct that enormous orchestra.
>
> "Now softly, softly, die away!" and the sounds obeyed him. "Now fuller, more joyful! Still more and more joyful!" And from an unknown depth rose increasingly triumphant sounds. "Now voices join in!" ordered Petya. And at first from afar he heard men's voices and then women's. The voices grew in harmonious

triumphant strength, and Petya listened to their surpassing beauty in awe and joy. (*W&P*, 1170–71)

We might note Tolstoy's technique here: the hissing of the whetstone against the metal is the only source of sound around Petya, so the music he hears and conducts is actually a profound metamorphosis of that sound. In effect, the beauty of Petya's music becomes semantically united with the notion of the sword, an instrument of death.

The next morning the attack begins, and Petya is shot clean through the head: "Petya was galloping along the courtyard, but, instead of holding the reins he waved his arms about rapidly and strangely, slipping farther and farther to the side in his saddle."[11] Thus music became death, with Petya still conducting his grand and joyful symphony. Before the attack, Pierre, a Russian prisoner, is sleeping among the French and dreaming of a huge watery globe with millions of droplets on it. Each of the droplets is trying to absorb the others, but sometimes they destroy it, and sometimes they merge with it; Pierre thinks that God is in the midst, and "each drop tries to expand so as to reflect Him to the greatest extent."[12] Tolstoy manipulates time so that we read this passage after we have heard Petya's music and seen him die. Thus the music is given a meaning related to the vision of the globe, and it unites the two heroes across the barrier of death.

At the end of the episode, Dolokhov watches the captured French pass by in file: "The French, excited by all that had happened, were talking loudly among themselves, but as they passed Dolokhov who gently switched his boots with his whip and watched them with cold glassy eyes that boded no good, they became silent" (*W&P*, 1183). Triumphant music, a globe that is God, and a procession of the dead. A juxtaposition of these three moments produces a rich complexity of implicit messages for the reader interpreting the entire novel, but for the characters—Petya, Pierre, and the captive French— they are but personal, self-enclosed experiences.

Another variant of enclosed spaces are worlds the reader perceives to be dominated, and thereby defined, by a single character. These worlds inevitably become the means of delineating that character as well. Anna Sherer's ballroom, where the novel begins, is one such world. In it she is less a person than a function of the novel, a means by which the upper-class society of Petersburg achieves existence and character. At other times, objects acquire more meaning than they would carry were they not marked as special identifying features of some character, and were they not set in contexts that then give them the enhanced meaning. Old Prince Bolkonsky's study bears his personal stamp in every detail, to the point where every object seems like a miniature Bolkonsky, aggressively insisting on his life principles: "The enormous study was full of things evidently in constant use. The large table covered with books and plans, the tall glass-fronted bookcases with keys in the locks, the high desk for writing while standing up, on which lay an open exercise book, and the lathe with tools laid ready to hand and shavings scattered around—all indicated continuous, varied and orderly activity" (*W&P*, 92).

This study is also Mary's torture chamber—she comes here every day at the appointed time to be humiliated over her geometry lessons. As Bolkonsky gets older and weaker, the study and all things in it also undergoes the same decline. At the time when the news from Austerlitz indicated that Andrey was killed there, we seem to be looking at three parallel deathward curves: the death of Andrey, of the old man's spirit, and of the room itself:

> When Princess Mary went to him at the usual hour he was working at his lathe and, as usual, did not look around at her.
> "Ah, Princess Mary!" he said suddenly in an unnatural voice, throwing down his chisel. (The wheel continued to revolve by its own impetus, and Princess Mary long remembered the dying creak of that wheel, which merged in her memory with what followed). (*W&P*, 346)

What followed was that Bolkonsky's own life ebbed away; he "walked less, ate less, slept less, and became weaker every day" (*W&P*, 348), and these stages of decay are but transformations of the dying sound of the wheel (incidentally, a kind of counterpart to the "ozheg-zheg" of Petya's sword). The wheel thus also becomes a funeral dirge for all his pride and intelligence. On a larger symbolic plane, the dying lathe and the fading Bolkonsky enact the curve of everyone's destiny.

A similar self-enclosed space belongs to "Uncle," whom the hunt-ing party visits at the end of the day (Book 7). His house is not overly clean, but it is not neglected, either, and "in the entry there was a smell of fresh apples, and wolf and fox skins hung about" (*W&P*, 560). The study "smelled strongly of tobacco and dogs." The resident household deity is Anisya, a stout woman full of hospitable dignity and cordiality. The tray of country fare she brings in has "a smack of Anisya Fedorovna herself: a savor of juiciness, cleanliness, whiteness and pleasant smiles" (*W&P*, 561). It all adds up to a description of "Uncle" himself, and he remains in our memory wrapped in a cocoon of odors of apples, tobacco, dogs, forming a world filled with the sound of his guitar, in the middle of which there is Natasha, dancing.

Sometimes such self-contained worlds are extended similes describing, as their counterpart, some particular place or situation in the plot. Thus Tolstoy describes Moscow, empty, awaiting Napoleon, in terms of a beehive. This space is determined not by the presence of one dominant figure, but by its absence, a notion just as dominant and all-important. It also has its own odor: "Instead of the former spiritu-ous fragrant smell of honey and venom, and the warm whiffs of crowded life, comes an odor of emptiness and decay mingling with the smell of honey" (*W&P*, 974). Similarly, "All is neglected and foul. Black robber bees are swiftly and stealthily prowling about the combs, and the short home bees, shriveled and listless as if they were old, creep slowly about without trying to hinder the robbers, having lost all motive and all sense of life" (*W&P*, 975). Every single detail of this long simile corresponds directly to the places and activities in the now "queenless" abandoned Moscow. Some have compared this metaphor to the description of Achilles' shield in *The Iliad*, but in fact Tolstoy's metaphor is a parody. The beehive metaphor is parodied by the busy well-run world of Anna Sherer's salon, for the beehive describes some-thing essentially dark and tragic, while the salon encloses a world of bustling stupidity.

Dushan Makovicky, Tolstoy's physician, records in his diary Tolstoy's notion of time and space. According to him Tolstoy thought "time and space can be described as human capabilities, but they make no sense as attributes of things."[13] This was because Tolstoy perceived time as nothing but "the human ability to perceive many things in one and the same space," a feat possible only through sequentiality, and space as the "human ability to perceive many things at the same time," which was possible only in the copresence of things. Both kinds of perceptions are needed for human beings to communicate with one another. And indeed, in *War and Peace*, time and space seem primarily a matter not of measurements, but of perceptions and relationships. Landscapes and interiors are important not in themselves, but because of the human presence from which they derive their meaning. Thus, when the Russian troops see the French by the river Enns on a clear autumn day, across a space of "some seven hundred yards," it is not the yardage that matters, but the fact that somewhere in that space there is an invisible line dividing life from death: "And what is there? Who is there?—there beyond that field, that tree, that roof lit up by the sun? No one knows, but one wants to know. You fear and yet long to cross that line, and know that sooner or later it must be crossed and you will have to find out what is there, just as you will inevitably have to learn what lies the other side of death" (*W&P*, 151–52). Thus space becomes meaningful as the encoding of our mortal condition. Ironically, as so often happens in *War and Peace* just before a battle, the sun is brilliant, and the landscape full of joyful excitement mingled with fear, again encoding an extremely complex human emotion, a simultaneous desire to live and perhaps to die.

The river itself—something we could metaphorically call time moving through space—functions in the landscape as the counterpart of streams of Russian troops trying to cross the bridge before the French can open fire on it. It becomes easy to think of human life as a river of no return. Just such a river is also part of the landscape at Bogucharovo, where, on a raft, Pierre and Andrey exchange ideas. Pierre believes that "in the universe, the whole universe, there is a kingdom of truth," and that he, Pierre, cannot vanish, has always existed, and always will exist (*W&P*, 421). In the meantime the river flows on and on into the evening, never to come back again, and the two friends move at right angles to this eternal stream, forcing their way across it while standing on a wooden human contraption, talking about meaning and hope. As for Andrey, he is thinking of his wife's death and his own guilt, which now cannot be redeemed. The scene, then, encapsulates Tolstoyan space and time, for in Pierre's and Andrey's special world of the moment, the science of physics, with its measurements, is irrelevant. As much as this time is special, in the novel it is also universal, and it seems to obliterate any difference between a book and the world.

6

Perspectives:
Author, Reader, Character

In *War and Peace* the world of lies and social amenities exists on the same plane as notions about power and value systems dependent on power, all of which represent the laws of history as conventionally understood. Tolstoy's own philosophy of history, his views on free will and determinism, exist in that other world of shared true feelings and fine perceptions, each of which starts an endless chain of consequences that continues to lengthen, becoming the force that shapes history. If we read the novel with our own sensitivities open to all the nuances of being that are experienced and shared by the characters, we will eventually see how Tolstoy the artist finds a way to insinuate Tolstoy the thinker into his characters, and into our minds as well, so that in the end the protagonists, Tolstoy, and ourselves will share the same or similar sets of values. This process denies us the distance needed for judging a character according to some logic of our own, but it also rewards us with an intimacy of mutual perceptions, so that what a character experiences also becomes a personal matter to us.

At the other end of this continuum we find the narrator speaking in his own voice. This voice is actually a complex design representing multiple relationships between itself and the many invented characters. According to R. F. Christian, "In most of the important episodes in *War and Peace* in which the major characters are involved, there is a subtle blend of author's narrative, outwardly spoken words and inwardly spoken thoughts; and it is in the many different combinations and variations of these three basic ingredients that Tolstoy's originality as a psychological realist lies" (Christian, 145). Christian took a closer look at these "many different variations" and saw an element of drama in Tolstoy's arrangement of dialogues between different characters, one intensified by another dramatic dialogue that goes on inside the characters themselves:

> One significant difference between the drafts and the definitive version is the much greater use Tolstoy makes in the matter of the principles of dramatization—the introduction in fact of dialogue, monologue and interior monologue into episodes which had first been written out in continuous narrative. The chapter about the doctor and his German wife, Mary Hendrikhovna,[1] was at first a mere paragraph without dialogue. It had dramatic possibilities and Tolstoy developed it scenically. There are numerous similar examples in *War and Peace*. But what is characteristically Tolstoyan is not the expansion of narrative into dialogue, but the changes rung on narrative, dialogue and monologue in order to express the true and innermost thoughts of the characters. People's thoughts, Tolstoy observed, are far more complex, erratic and unpredictable than people's actions. (Christian, 142–43)

The inner conversation of characters with themselves is not exactly the twentieth-century stream of consciousness in which disjointed fragments of impressions float through a character's mind. It resembles more an ordered exchange between sets of perceptions that accumulate into a coherent universe within the mind; this universe then seeks out points of contact with other individual universes, a process that constitutes the "outer" dialogue. Superimposed upon these processes is the larger frame of ongoing dialogue between the author and the reader. This superimposition produces a double effect: As we watch the characters trying to understand and shape their lives, we also hear the author-narrator commenting on the process, explaining things, and giving us more information than the characters can perceive at a given moment. That author does not speak with a single unchanging voice, however. His message changes from absolute, unappealable assertions to barely perceptible whispers of someone drowned in the noise of other voices.

The extreme absolute position of the author, according to Gary Saul Morson, is a language governed by nonfictive speech genres, since it claims "literal, not literary, truth" (Morson, 19). It is a language not addressed to anyone; it simply states what is. Consequently, a distinction is formed between "dialogic" language, which speaks to some audience and expects an answer, and "absolute" language, which "does not say; it is a saying. Admitting no authorship, it condescends to no dialogue." It is like the language of God, "absolute and unconditional in the sense that, unlike the utterance of a person, it is not a function of the circumstances that evoked it, and its meaning is not qualified by an audience whose potential reactions have to be taken into account. When spoken, it belongs to no one; when written it is Scripture" (Morson, 14).

One example of such language in the novel could be the opening of Book 9: "On the twelfth of June, 1812, the forces of Western Europe crossed the Russian frontier and war began, that is, an event took place opposed to human reason and to human nature" (*W&P*, 667). The Tolstoyan "that is" does not come across as an opinion, but as a given fact that precludes all discussion. You cannot say, "But I don't believe war is opposed to human nature!" because Tolstoy's comment is not a question of belief—as a statement, it is what it is. Most of the main assertions in the nonfictional parts of the novel are in this language, and it is no wonder that many critics thought these parts did not belong in the novel, since a novel by its nature represents, and is, a complex multiple dialogue about life. Nevertheless, this absolute language does apply to human feelings and thus also to events and their meaning in the novel, and therefore constitutes a dialogue of its own kind with the reader. If war is as Tolstoy sees it, then those engaged in it—not only Napoleon and Kutuzov, but also Andrey, Rostov, and all the others—have lost their reason and are acting against their own nature as human beings, and by extension, whatever they do has a criminal aspect to it, whether they know it or not. All other activities of the characters, even in the intervals of peace, must then bear the stain of that absolute judgment.

The novel can also be read as an account of how one could remain, or become, rational and human in an existential frame that does not readily permit such characteristics. It may indeed be Tolstoy's main task as a novelist, but not as a thinker or judge of history, to lead us to the realization that we are human in a way that does not make us criminals in spite of what history makes us do. There is a moment, for instance, when Nikolay Rostov and his squadron attack a French cavalry detachment and take a prisoner who is "fair and young, with a dimple in the chin and light-blue eyes" (*W&P*, 725). Praised by his superiors, Rostov cannot shake a "vaguely disagreeable feeling of moral nausea" over what he did, how he slashed at the young French officer with his sword, even if he did not kill him. "I remember how my arm paused when I raised it," thinks Rostov, and this is just the minute point, the fraction of a second in the swirls of history in which Rostov's humanity lives. Looking at Tolstoy's metaphor about free will and determinism, we can think of the earth in its roundness as history, and of the flat slice of it circumscribed by our horizon, within which we see for ourselves, as the individual experience representing our free will. When Rostov hesitates, and when he feels the moral nausea, he is human and free in a little world circumscribed by that experience.

Morson also mentions a different kind of absolute language in the novel, namely, that of proverbs. "Like biblical commands," says Morson, "they can be attributed to no particular human author. . . . Proverbs are never spoken, they are only cited; and to cite a proverb is to make its nonhistorical statement applicable to, but in no sense conditioned by, a particular historical situation. It is, rather, the historical situation that reveals its conformity to the timeless pattern described by the proverb" (Morson, 14). One character who represents this timeless pattern is the cheerful, round Platon Karataev, whose entire discourse is like an unbroken stream of spontaneous Russian proverbs spoken impersonally and related not to the given events of the time, but to that timeless stream of being that surrounds us all.[2] Such extension of our humanity to the point where it can no longer be quantified is achieved not when we separate ourselves from the globelike, deterministic roundness of history, but when our individuality becomes dissolved in it.[3]

Whatever shape Tolstoy's authority takes, whether an unnamed source of absolute statements or an inarticulate peasant who can't put a sentence together and therefore speaks nothing but the absolute truth, the author was aware that "nothing more arrogant can be said than that the words spoken by me are uttered through me by God" (Morson, 26). So, to reduce his arrogance, Tolstoy becomes the godlike speaker through his narrator, or, more specifically, his two narrators. One narrator makes his presence clearly felt, almost as if he were sitting opposite the reader in an easy chair, with the novel between them. He likes to chat with us directly, to explain things, to give, as it were, a briefing before raising the curtain for action. In Book 10 we are told a great many things about the upcoming Battle of Borodino, about Napoleon's dispositions for it, and about how they were not and could not possibly have been carried out—there is even a little map that Tolstoy drew when he visited the site. Later in the book this narrator proceeds to argue about history in relation to the general human condition. He becomes insistent, persuasive, and claims more and more space for himself as the novel proceeds, until at the end, in the first and especially the second epilogue, he clearly becomes the dominant, if not the only, voice. He is also the one who utters Tolstoy's absolute statements, often as part of his argument.

The other narrator seems mindful of his conventional responsibilities. He does not intrude upon the scene, keeps himself invisible and does not usurp the characters' domain, except at such (rather frequent) times when he hovers behind his characters' backs and whispers to the reader what so-and-so really meant or intended when he or she said or did something. This is guidance not by straight argument but by discreet information. In fact, his discretion is often so great that he does not appear to be saying anything opinionated at all. Things are simply happening before our eyes as if there were no narrator. Yet, even then this invisible and omniscient teller of the tale does make his point by manipulating both information and situations and also by generous use of various extended metaphors that lead us to understand the events in one particular way—his way, of course. Thus Tolstoy succeeds in making the narrative discourse function in effect as expository.

We already saw this device working in the description of Natasha at the opera. A similar device requires a character to be present at a given scene so that Tolstoy can describe it through that character's eyes in a manner calculated to carry Tolstoy's own views. On one occasion he uses Prince Andrey to convey the ideas on history and causality specifically articulated in the epilogues and elsewhere in the novel. Andrey is a witness at the war council before the episode at Austerlitz, and what we read is what he, and not the narrator, sees and hears.

The scene is remarkable for the absence of the most important aspect of a war council—namely, a description of the actual plans for the coming engagement. What Andrey sees at first is the mud-bespattered and excited General Weyrother, fresh from the field, and the sleepy Kutuzov, who had told Andrey earlier that the battle is going to be lost. This contrast alone makes all the planning meaningless, and Kutuzov confirms the futility of the council by snoring through the proceedings. What Andrey hears are not statements about action plans, but a whole string of Austrian place-names that in the end produce an impression of nonsensical gibberish: Kobelnitz, Sokolnitz, again Sokolnitz and Kobelnitz, then Schlappanitz and Thuerassa, and Schlappanitz and Bellowitz, and so on (*W&P*, 280).

What Andrey sees is not serious generals engaged in an important conference, but a set of figures whose expressions and bearing have no relation to the topic at hand. Incidentally, most of the generals have foreign names, the sounds of which accompany the gibberish of Schlappanitz and Bellowitz. First Miloradovich looks meaningfully at everyone, but nobody can interpret his glances.[4] Then, next to Weyrother, Count Langeron rapidly twists a snuffbox in his hands, Przebyszewski holds his hand to his ear, and tall, blond general Buxhövden fixes his eyes on a burning candle. In the meantime, Kutuzov sleeps and Andrey dreams of the glorious feats he will accomplish in the next day's battle. Ironically, the next morning finds Andrey lying wounded on his back, looking at the clouds and understanding the meaninglessness of it all.

Andrey is also a witness, much later, at the war council at Drissa, where we can watch through his eyes the Russian and German generals discussing how to stop Napoleon's invasion. The entire scene is much more complex than the council at Austerlitz, but the basic device is the same: A narrator describes not what happens, but what someone perceives is happening, which, in turn, is what Tolstoy would like us to think is the truth. Here, through Andrey's thoughts, Tolstoy expands upon his own ideas, as we also see them in the epilogues, about war and the sense or nonsense of planning things. Andrey's impressions about the council are actually foreshadowed at the beginning of Book 9, where Tolstoy as narrator expounds on the causes of wars and concludes that any identifiable cause is just as valid and just as false as any other, and that events in history are but realizations of some of these accumulated causes, but not of others. These events are random, beyond logic, and uncontrollable; in essence, kings are but history's slaves.

At times Tolstoy's narrator does not even articulate the thoughts or feelings of a character, but tries instead to make us aware of them by a straight narrative description of objects at hand. The Russian critic A. A. Saburov cites a passage in which the narrator's voice seems absent or neutral, but carries an implicit message nevertheless (Saburov, 578–79). In Book 1 (the year is 1805) Andrey sets off to war after having quarreled with his father. Tolstoy describes his packing in the plainest possible terms, but just the same, the choice of objects described, and their origin, carries an emotional load of hidden, fiercely controlled tension between these two loving and proud men: "The old prince, not altering his routine, retired as usual after dinner. The little princess [Andrey's wife Lisa] was in her sister-in-law's room. . . . Only those things he always kept with him remained in his room; a small box, a large canteen fitted with silver plate, two Turkish pistols and a saber—a present from his father who had brought it from the siege of Ochakov. All these travelling effects of Prince Andrew were in very good order: new, clean, and in cloth covers carefully tied with tapes" (*W&P*, 107–8). The good order of the traveling effects underlines Andrey's disturbed emotions at this moment. He is going to war (and possibly his death) without being able to show his father the love he feels for him.[5] This notion is reinforced by Prince Bolkonsky's equally orderly, and equally painful, retreat to his room after dinner. And so, in the end we learn not about boxes and sabers, but about the self-destructive love and pride that marks the characters of both father and son and that in the ultimate reckoning leaves them with little else to do in the novel except die. Thus the narrator's calm descriptive voice maps the logic for future tragic events.

In this oblique, masked narrator's discourse we are led to perceive Tolstoy's position not by what the narrator might argue, but by how he arranges events before our eyes. The battle of Schöngraben is an example. According to Tolstoy's argument, as an unnatural and criminal event, the battle should have nothing at all to do with natural processes, but as a human experience through which to seek redemption, it is described in a sustained parallel between the human actors and the living earth. For illustration, we may select a certain sequence of events from the entire description of the battle. First Prince Andrey sees a soldier being punished for stealing (W&P, 186). The soldier is naked, and two other soldiers hold him down on the ground while still two others are strike him regularly with switches. The man screams in an "unnatural" voice while the punishing officer, even more unnaturally, reads him a sermon about how a soldier is supposed to be a brave and honest man, not a thief. A young officer, a bystander, looks at Andrey "with a bewildered and pained expression on his face" (W&P, 186) but the narrator gives us no hint as to Andrey's feelings as he rides by. Since the world of the novel consists of characters' perceptions, this lack of expected feeling might surprise us, but it also tells us something chilling about Andrey; it is one of the early hints of the cosmic indifference, soon reinforced by the Austerlitz sky, that later envelops him on his deathbed. Tolstoy fills the empty space in our minds where Andrey's feeling should be with the image of a suffering body pressed down into the ground, almost blended with the earth. Just a little while later, while the soldiers are drinking vodka and philosophizing about death and the afterlife, a French cannonball strikes the ground:

"Some herb vodka? Certainly!" said Tushin. "but still, to conceive a future life . . ."

He did not finish. Just then there was a whistle in the air; nearer and nearer, faster and louder, louder and faster, a cannon ball, as if it had not finished saying what was necessary, thudded into the ground near the shed with superhuman force, throwing up a mass of earth. The ground seemed to groan at the terrible impact. (*W&P*, 189)

The naked soldier being flogged on the ground, the cannonball smashing into the earth, and the earth's subsequent groaning form links in a single chain, a single discourse.[6] A single action becomes a totality, and a voice becomes a configuration in the vast organism of reality. Similarly, at the end of the battle the Russian troops retreat with their wounded like a spacious and tragic flow, a moaning river in the night: "In the darkness, it seemed as though a gloomy unseen river was flowing always in one direction, humming with whispers and talk and the sound of hoofs and wheels. Amid the general rumble, the groans and voices of the wounded were more distinctly heard than any other sound in the darkness of the night. The gloom that enveloped the army was filled with their groans, which seemed to melt into one with the darkness of the night."[7] Tolstoy develops this almost mythological aura of an all-encompassing oneness of the single organism Earth in his narrator's voice, giving no hint that any of the characters involved—Nikolai Rostov, Captain Tushin, Andrey, Kutuzov, or Bagration—are aware of it. The result is that the narrator and his readers, standing outside the frame of the narrative, know more about the implications of this unity than do the participants themselves, although the basic fabric of the story is woven by individual perceptions and their accompanying limitations.

Sometimes a seemingly neutral description of objects and circumstances contains not only a foreshadowing of future events, but also a judgment of the value systems that brought them about. Pierre's first encounter with the Freemason Bazdeev is one such instance. In Book 5, after his stupid duel with Dolokhov, Pierre is deeply depressed and cannot perceive any meaning in his life. In this state he travels to Petersburg, repeatedly asking himself unanswerable questions: "What is bad? What is good? What should one love and what hate? What does one live for? And what am I? What is life and what is death? What power governs all?"[8] The narrator makes these questions physically palpable by his simile of the screw: "It was as if the thread of the chief screw which held his life together were stripped, so that the screw could not get in or out, but went on turning uselessly in the same place" (*W&P*, 377). Thus having attuned our minds to objects serving as symbols for a mental state, the narrator proceeds to describe the things and people inside the relay station at which Pierre is going to change horses.[9] Here we find a postmaster, his wife, the valet, and a peasant woman selling Torzhok embroidery. Pierre cannot understand how they can all go on living without solving the problems that absorb him, while in the meantime, as if by way of her solution, the peasant woman keeps trying to sell him useless things, like goatskin slippers, "in a whining voice" that seems to degrade Pierre's deep dark thoughts to a similar sour whine. As the stripped screw keeps turning, a new traveler appears. He is a "short, large-boned, yellow-faced, wrinkled old man" with a "gloomy and tired face" and "with a pair of felt boots on his thin bony legs," and he has a servant "who was also a yellow, wrinkled old man, without beard or mustache, evidently not because he was shaven but because they had never grown" (*W&P*, 379). This looks like a new, extended metaphor for Pierre's pointlessly hopeless condition. The wrinkled yellow faces seem reminiscent of embalmed corpses, perhaps of some great men that were important in a distant time. The thin and bony legs in the cumbersome felt boots create a picture that mocks the grand fairy-tale visions of heroes in seven-league boots traversing fantastic distances toward some noble goal. The beardless face of the valet clearly suggests that he may be a eunuch, a fruitless living corpse. We certainly do not expect anything positive from these two men, anything that could help resolve Pierre's quandary. And yet this new traveler, Bazdeev, has a stern, clever face; he breaks through Pierre's despair, shows him a shining path to the future, and becomes his Masonic mentor. What is Bazdeev's Freemasonry worth after such an introduction? We begin to suspect very strongly that all his teaching is nonsense, and this suspicion is confirmed at Pierre's initiation into the order, described in Pierre's own perceptions as a grotesque comedy. Furthermore, the nonsensical nature of this entire mystical doctrine is made altogether evident later in the novel, when Pierre deduces from it that he is predestined to kill Napoleon because his own name and nationality written in French, albeit a little misspelled as "L'russe Besuhof," produce a mystical numerical value equal to that of Napoleon, perceived by the Freemasons as the Beast of the Apocalypse: 666.[10]

We must also note that the negative images in the stagecoach station are not presented to us as Pierre's observations but through the narrator's own eyes, for otherwise there would be no logic to Pierre's later infatuation with the teaching and rituals of the Masonic order. The narrator has given us a perspective of Pierre of which the character himself is unaware at that moment.

In the Tolstoyan worldview, as it emerges in the novel, the Masons are wrong for similar reasons as the German theoretician-generals, the great reformer Speransky, and even Andrey himself in his eagerness to propose plans for upcoming battles and designing laws for military reform. All such efforts are based on the presumption that human reason, by exercising its capacity to make abstract designs, can produce valid models of reality in any sphere. Whatever is false, useless, and harmful in human activity stems from such a presumption.[11] The real essence of things has nothing to do with abstract models, but rather with those processes in nature that can only be misunderstood if we try to define or quantify them; nonetheless, they can be recognized instinctively, in some deep layer of the soul. Another of Tolstoy's narrative methods entails sharing privileged knowledge with the reader. The characters express points of view that reveal their inner worlds in a manner of which they are not conscious, but thanks to the narrator, the reader recognizes these aspects of the characters' psyches and is thus able to pass judgment soundly.

This technique stands in direct opposition to Tolstoy's other main device—representing the author's truth in terms of the characters' own perceptions. An example presents itself in a particular moment in the conversation between Pierre and Andrey during Pierre's visit in Bogucharovo, where Andrey lives after his return from captivity and just before he meets Natasha. Pierre, talking with Andrey about his duel with Dolokhov, thanks God that he did not kill his combatant. Andrey answers that "to kill a vicious dog is a very good thing really," and we may take this as his opinion of Dolokhov. A moment later Andrey says that remorse and illness are the only two evils he knows, and also that now he lives only for himself; nonetheless, his idea of "himself" includes both his sister and father. Neither Pierre nor Andrey can know what Dolokhov said to Nikolay Rostov after the duel. Laying wounded in the sleigh, Dolokhov expressed great concern about his mother and sister,[12] and to his surprise Nikolay learned that "Dolokhov the brawler, Dolokhov the bully, lived in Moscow with his mother and a hunchback sister, and was the most affectionate of sons and brothers."[13] This is also the same Dolokhov who had nothing but utter contempt for the rest of the human race. We as readers may be somewhat surprised to understand that by calling Dolokhov a "vicious dog," Andrey has in some sense unknowingly characterized himself. Nonetheless, if we are merciful, we can say that Andrey's remarks about loving no one but himself and those who are his own measure not his character, but his despair.

The wisdom gleaned by Andrey under the Austerlitz sky is a heavy burden to him, for it tells him of the utter inconsequentiality of all our ambitions, dreams, and commitments. Pierre even notices a mark upon Andrey's face which from our privileged distance we recognize as the first shadow of his coming death, namely, the "wrinkle on his brow indicating prolonged concentration on some one thought" (W&P, 414). This mark gives Andrey a look of "preoccupation and despondency"—precisely what he looks like as he lays dying after Borodino. We know the "one thought" that engages him, while those who love him do not—simply put, it is the inconsequentiality of life and the omnipresent goodness of death.

Perhaps the earliest intimation of Andrey's deep-seated and perhaps unconscious alienation from life comes when we first see him entering Madame Sherer's salon with his half-closed, bored eyes and his evident contempt for everybody except Pierre. The contrast between Pierre's enthusiasm for life and Andrey's coldness suggests a symbolic encounter between the impersonations of life and death, and this structural principle holds true throughout the entire novel. In this context the friendship between Pierre and Andrey carries the tremendous symbolic load of resolution of our intolerable existential dilemma, of the eventual unity of death and life. When we first read this passage, we cannot, of course, be conscious of such parameters, but as we move forward through the book, and as the destinies of the two protagonists unfold, the metaphor becomes more and more clear.

Andrey's concentrated thought begins to envelop him as an ultimate knowledge as he lies wounded after the Battle of Borodino. The first, dramatic confrontation at the beginning of the battle is between a spinning, smoking cannonball and Andrey's sudden rush of passionate love of life as he watches it. Later, death comes as a gesture of compassion: The doctor, who knows that Andrey cannot survive, kisses him tenderly on the lips. At that moment "all the best and happiest moments of his life— especially his earliest childhood, when he used to be undressed and put to bed, and when leaning over him his nurse sang him to sleep[14] and he, burying his head in the pillow, felt happy in the mere consciousness of life—returned to his memory, not merely as something past but as something present" (*W&P*, 907). So, the doctor's kiss of death turns the memory of life into an immediate, real presence, and Andrey "felt like weeping childlike, kindly and almost happy tears." As we can see, the meaning of the passage comes not from what the doctor did, but from what Andrey felt and remembered.

Andrey's delirium after the battle, in Mytishchi (*W&P*, 1021ff.), is depicted as an altered state of mind due to the trauma of his wound. Yet we must also remember that Andrey's condition is equivalent to a single individual's consciousness of the trauma inflicted upon the entire country by the onslaught of Napoleon's armies. Tolstoy portrays Russia itself as a huge organism that has received a tremendous and potentially mortal wound: Napoleon is in Moscow, the city is burning, and the Russian army is almost decimated. In this way an individual and the world around him are so linked that each can function as a metaphor for the other, and this is one of the principles governing the construction of the entire novel. This principle also extends to the condition of the other two main characters, Pierre and Natasha. The world surrounding Pierre changes in his mind to resemble an apocalyptic text in which absurd notions, like his destiny as "l'russe

Besuhof," function as if in a dream, according to their own logic, and although incoherent in the light of ordinary thinking, they are somehow a part of another network, a deep structure underlying and governing the dynamics of the novel. Thus Pierre's state of mind, and that of Andrey in his delirium, become symbolic equivalents of one another as they extend in the larger framework, to the condition of the whole country. At the same time Natasha, recovering from the trauma of her misadventure with Kuragin and Dolokhov, also enters a different state of mind, where at least one new thing becomes visible, namely, that Pierre is in love with her. She also learns that Andrey is among the Russian wounded in Rostov's own convoy. Andrey and Pierre thus become two counterpoints in a space we might call "love," which in turn is juxtaposed with a vast new expanse we can think of as death. We can also observe Natasha's altered state of mind as she enters the shadowy room in which Andrey lies. With his raised knees, he looks to her for a moment like a "horrible body," and she feels how "something heavy was beating rhythmically against all the walls of the room: it was her own heart, sinking with alarm and terror and overflowing with love" (W&P, 1019). Thus Andrey in his delirium, although alone with himself, is also the focal point of concentric circles representing altered states of consciousness in ever-widening frames of reference that become, as Tolstoy put it, "the unsettled question of life and death, which hung not only over Bolkonsky but over all Russia" (W&P, 1025).

Within these circles Andrey's broken thoughts, acting "apart from his will," turn constantly around something that at first seems like a yearning for the Gospels and then acquires an intermittent focus as "a happiness of the soul alone, the happiness of loving" (W&P, 1022). We then see a strange and ominous process: On the one hand, what seemed at first like an undefined oppressive presence in the room becomes a sort of white "shirtlike sphinx," and then a sphinx with the pale face of Natasha, and finally Natasha herself, to whom he can say "I love you." On the other hand, the very idea of love, as it becomes more clear, moves away from any object toward a feeling that is "the essence of the soul" and does not require a living world around it. So, ironically, as Andrey and Natasha come together again, he is at the same time somewhere else, at some other center of the mind, altogether on his own.

The name of this special solitude is death. We read about Andrey's last days after we have already witnessed Pierre's frantic and terrible hours in Moscow, in which he wanders through the streets, attempts to save a child from the fire, is finally taken prisoner by the French, and is made to witness the execution of young Moscow "incendiaries," whereupon he loses all faith in God. As we recall this episode, both Natasha and Mary, Andrey's sister, perceive to their horror that Andrey has "changed," softened somehow, and that this softening and gentleness are signs of approaching death. There is a "calm almost antagonistic look" (1084) in his eyes, and he must make an effort to be affectionate to his son Nicholas, Mary, and Natasha, for he sees that they no longer matter, "because something else, much more important, had been revealed to him" (*W&P*, 1085). The revelation is that he, Andrey, is a particle of love who is about to return to the eternal source, and any attachment to particular individuals only hinders what must be. Here, of course, Andrey achieves the concept of Pierre's vision of the globe with the little drops of water—individual lives—merging and sinking into the depths of the total entity, so that both characters reach the same epiphany, one at the door of death and the other at the door of new life. Indeed, a pattern of visions and perceptions shapes the meaning of the plot, if not the plot itself: Without their coming to the same ultimate insight, Pierre's liberation from the French and Andrey's death would have meant nothing at all.

Thus, Andrey's conversation with Pierre on the raft in Bogucharovo, with the river of life flowing beneath them, is meaningful as an inevitable point in the overall pattern of their relationship and, by necessary extension, the relationship between death and life. For Andrey their meeting was the turning point of restored hope and belief in the possibility of happiness: "His meeting with Pierre formed an epoch in Prince Andrew's life. Though outwardly he continued to live in the same old way, inwardly he began a new life" (*W&P*, 423). His new feelings were soon powerfully reinforced by his encounter with Natasha, from which grew in his heart the new rosebud of love. Tolstoy marks the turn in his life with an extended metaphor,

Andrey's two encounters with an ancient oak tree that grew on the way to Otradnoe, the Rostovs' estate.

In this episode, Tolstoy reverts to the character's perspective, presenting a world experienced not by the narrator but by Andrey himself. And it is interesting that Andrey perceives nature in the way that sentimental writers might, by ascribing human qualities to it. In springtime, on the way to Otradnoe, the dejected Andrey looks at a giant oak that had not yet put out its green leaves: "'Spring, love, happiness!' this oak seemed to say. 'Are you not weary of that stupid, meaningless, constantly repeated fraud? Always the same and always a fraud! There is no spring, no sun, no happiness! . . . Yes, the oak is right, a thousand times right,' thought Prince Andrew" (*W&P*, 459). On the way back on that same road, totally rejuvenated in spirit by his encounter with Natasha, Andrey passes by the oak again, this time in full bloom, and thinks to himself, "'Yes, here in this forest was that oak with which I agreed. . . . Yes, it is the same oak,' thought Prince Andrew, and all at once he was seized by an unreasoning springtime feeling of joy and renewal" (*W&P*, 462).

What matters is not that Tolstoy seems to contradict himself by letting Andrey have notions similar to those of a sentimental writer; the point is elsewhere: Andrey was lonely at the time, and therefore felt very acutely that he was something other than nature and people. The painful, poignant need to break through this otherness and solitude led Andrey to start his imaginary dialogue with the oak. That dialogue is very revealing: We see from it that Andrey feels he is old (at the age of 31), that he is scarred by life, and yet, deeper than that, that he is somehow strong and tragic, and therefore someone worthy of admiration and pity. He seeks the solace of the tree, but it is also clear that he is in the right frame of mind to fall in love with the impish, happy Natasha. It is also evident that this proud world-weary man is, and in his heart has always been, a poet. This last realization makes clear that it has been the author-narrator's voice all along, silent in and of itself, yet eloquent through Andrey, that has structured the deep layers of his soul, his response to life at this turning point, and our own idea of who Andrey really is.

We might at this point indulge the idea that Tolstoy, who could tell us so much about Andrey and ourselves, must have been a bit of a poet himself. At the very least he was in part a poet when his authorial voice spoke in extended metaphors to further the narration. Here again we come to this characteristic of Tolstoy: What appears to be just an image, background sketch, or philosophical reflection functions in essence as a continuation of the narrative discourse, conveying action.

We come across one such extended metaphor at the beginning of the book, at Anna Sherer's party. Tolstoy is faced with the problem of group dynamics; he must manage this large crowd of worldly people to make them function like a smooth machine:

> And having got rid of this young man who did not know how to behave [Pierre] she resumed her duties as hostess and continued to listen and watch, ready to help at any point where the conversation might happen to flag. As the foreman of a spinning mill, when he has set the hands to work, goes round and notices here a spindle that has stopped, or there one that creaks or makes more noise than it should, and hastens to check the machine and to set it in proper motion, so Anna Pavlovna moved about her drawing room, approaching now a silent, now a too-noisy group, and by a word or slight rearrangement kept the conversational machine in steady, proper and regular motion." (*W&P*, 10)

Everything in the scene is constantly turning, everything is in motion, nothing is human: spindles, wheels, a conversational machine. Then we suddenly realize that this scene is a vicious, and for this reason hilarious parody of history, in which the "foremen" of this world—kings, emperors, and other assorted "great men"—imagine themselves in charge. The machine can only work when it is a machine, and not a community of souls; this we learn from the Petersburg society, in which no one even expects to be believed.

Within this metaphor of a spinning mill, Tolstoy inserts another: people as edibles, whose importance is measured by their worth in culinary terms. At each of her parties Madame Sherer has someone who can serve as a centerpiece of sorts, someone reputed to be very clever, or charming, or rich and powerful, or all these things at once, around whom the whole mill can efficiently turn. In this episode she has two such figures, Abbé Morio and Vicomte de Mortemart: "As a clever maître d'hôtel serves up as a specially choice delicacy a piece of meat that no one who had seen it in the kitchen would have cared to eat, so Anna Pavlovna served up to her guests, first the vicomte and then the abbé, as peculiarly choice morsels. . . . The vicomte was served up to the company in the choicest and most advantageous style, like a well-garnished joint of roast beef on a hot dish" (*W&P*, 10–11). One might call this scene a "judgmental trope"—it not only makes characters more vivid, but also passes a negative judgment that colors our perception. A vicomte made of roast beef and an abbé made of something that does not go down very well satirize worldliness, intelligence, and charm, indeed, civilization itself. Clearly, Tolstoy's epilogues concerning war, peace, history, freedom, and the nature of society have their beginnings here.

The culinary trope in the shape of the well-worn cliché of cannon fodder is applied to the bathing soldiers of Andrey's regiment on their retreat from Smolensk. There is also a connection between the group dynamics among both the partygoers in Mme. Sherer's ballroom and the soldiers on the battlefield. For instance, Sherer as a mill foreman has her counterpart in General Bagration, the commander of Russian troops at Schöngraben. The contrast is complete not only in the settings of peace and war, but also in the styles of leadership. As much as Sherer is anxious about every little detail and keeps total control of the situation, Bagration acquiesces to whatever the various messengers tell him, knowing very well (even if unconsciously) that a battle is a chaotic event without any system or rules. There is only one thing the battlefield commander can do: Make the soldiers and officers under his command feel as though he both knows what is going on and can safely bring them to the end of the battle through his superior knowledge. Says the narrator: "Prince Andrew noticed that though what happened was due to chance and was independent of the commander's will, owing to the tact Bagration showed, his presence was very valuable. Officers who approached him with disturbed countenances became calm; soldiers and officers greeted him gaily, grew more cheerful in his presence, and were evidently anxious to display their courage before him" (*W&P*, 193).

The two opposed philosophies of leadership correspond perfectly to the entire structure of events in the novel as well as to the basic outlines of Tolstoy's philosophical argument. Though separated by time and space and by the nature of surrounding events, Sherer's "workshop" and Bagration's battleground are nevertheless closely linked together in a sort of "bridge of direct relevance" that may be part of the novel's overall design.

In conclusion, one can say that Tolstoy does not so much speak in many different author's voices as he does in many modulations of a single voice—the voice that tells us that life is infinitely complex and that we will never begin to reach the sort of full knowledge of it that could inform our moral decisions, but that we must make these decisions nevertheless based our sense of personal responsibility for any given moment. In that way we become rooted in a wide and generous acceptance of life as it comes to us.

7

Recurrences and Linkages

Prince Andrey's two imaginary dialogues with the oak tree show us the change in his perception of the world, caused by his meeting with Natasha; at the same time, and for unrelated reasons, nature in springtime was changing as well. The oak had nothing at all to do with Natasha, but in our own minds, as in Andrey's, a link has been established. We could speak of "narrative rhyming" in the sense that, as in verse, two juxtaposed but otherwise unrelated elements generate an additional meaning that would not exist otherwise.[1] In *War and Peace* often two or more separate events are so configured that they create an echo of each other in our minds. At particular points in the novel this echo creates a new level of meaning, perhaps an awareness of a law of causality in some different dimension of the text, or an ironic frame of the events described between the two echoes, or a sudden poignancy and depth of insight to a given situation. Taken in their entirety, these narrative rhymes compose a network of cross-references and complex narrative patterns that in its own way amounts to a well-shaped structure that affects the entire work. Victor Shklovsky refers to Tolstoy's "metonymic method," whereby the writer gives us a close-up of one part of some entity—a physical detail, or a delicate shade of emotion—

so that having believed that part, we also perceive the whole as real (Shklovsky, 400). We can advance this insight further: As some of the parts become interlinked, they function like literary isotopes, marking the level and the potential of a given narrative line. We also come to think of these linkages as "real," that is, as forces shaping the body of the novel, even if their causal relationships in the flow of narration seem quite arbitrary or even altogether absent.

Many of these narrational isotopes exist in three distinct categories. One grouping pertains to given focal points. These may be particular places or objects around which a series of significant events take place. We may think, for instance, of the couch in old Prince Bolkonsky's study, on which he sometimes slept. After Andrey leaves for the front, the prince, evidently upset over the hostile parting from his son, becomes restless and keeps changing the places in which he sleeps, finding them all unsatisfactory. Worst of all these locales is "his customary couch in the study. That couch was dreadful to him, probably because of the oppressive thoughts he had when lying there" (*W&P*, 771). These thoughts have to do with his irritable, angry love for his daughter, whom he always had a compulsion to persecute, a situation exacerbated by his increasing reliance on her. After suffering a stroke while making preparations to confront the advancing French, the prince ("a little old man in a uniform and decorations") is carried to his study and laid down "on the very couch he had so feared of late" (*W&P*, 795). Having said so many unjust things to his daughter, Prince Bolkonsky, crippled by the stroke, is physically unable to pronounce the words of apology and love he now yearns to say. At this point the couch is not just an object, but a signifier, a focal point of many contradictory, poignant emotions, the carrier of both a pathetic, unjust anger and a pathetic, helpless remorse. Taken from Bald Hills to Bogucharovo, the half-paralyzed prince keeps trying to say something, but no one comprehends his meaning (his proud anger had been so convincing that no one imagines he might be straining to articulate an apology). Princess Mary, looking at her father and oblivious to his desire to say he loves her, thinks involuntarily about his death and connects that event with rebirth of hope for her own life. Needless to say, she immediately feels guilty and then bears this guilt like a stone in her heart, especially when the old prince finally manages to convey his love to her just before his death. Even though these events occur away from Bald Hills, the complex of emotions associated with the couch there remains the same in this new setting, except that now, ironically, the previous object of the emotions, Mary, is now their bearer. Therefore it seems quite logical that after her father's funeral Mary would be lying on a sofa thinking of the inevitability of death and "of her own baseness, which she had not suspected, but which had shown itself during her father's illness" (*W&P*, 807).

Even before these events, the themes of parent and child, and life and death, as they pertain to Andrey and his wife Lise, are shaped around a "large leather sofa" in Andrey's study in Bald Hills (*W&P*, 349). This sofa is being carried to Lise's bedroom in preparation for her childbirth, but its heavy, large blackness strongly evokes the image of a coffin. Tolstoy helps turn our thoughts in this direction by noting that the servants carrying the sofa had "a quiet and solemn look," like those of pallbearers. It could well be the same sofa on which the old prince thought his bad thoughts—at the very least, it is the same object on the symbolic level of interconnections—and Lise does actually die on it while giving birth to Andrey's son.[2] As is often the case in *War and Peace*, none of the protagonists are in the least aware of the sofa as a symbol. For them it is simply a familiar piece of furniture that may have some emotions associated with it. The characters cannot know of the network of significations, extending beyond the actual course of their lives, which such objects represent for the reader. Reading about the "quiet and solemn look" of the servants carrying the sofa, for instance, one is suddenly reminded of the serious expression on the peasants' faces just before the Battle of Borodino, expressions that show an awareness of the "solemnity of the impending moment" and "that spoke not of personal matters but of the universal questions of life and death" (*W&P*, 854). The triviality of a single human life and death, as represented by the sofa, is contrasted with the panorama of historical events, and through this connection is elevated to a position of equivalence with them. The personal and the suprapersonal blend into one.

There are many similar linkages in the novel. In terms of the unfolding of events, these links could be called "signs of destiny." Albert Cook gives several good examples from Book 1, in which situations that at first seem inconsequential actually constitute hints of future developments, a device that creates an overall impression of destiny:

> There is a meaning portentously present, though the meaning is not yet. People are brought mysteriously into each other's orbits; as Prince Vassily carries on the conversation which will culminate in Anatole's unsuccessful overture for Marya, the stupid Julie Karagina writes portentously of a man, Nikolai Rostov, unknown to her correspondent, who will at last, through the transformations of war, become Marya's fitting husband. . . . Then will Pierre be liberated to marry the girl he will love from Book Eight on, though here, in Book One, he scarcely dreams, sitting across from her at a dinner party, that the thin thirteen-year-old could possibly become of such absorbing interest. Yet he must have some intimation of this future, or why otherwise at her look has he "felt an impulse to laugh himself without knowing why?" (W&P, 1402)

There are certainly more such fine signals in the novel. We could think, for instance, of the corpulent civilian, an accountant, who is permitted to indulge his curiosity by viewing the Battle of Schöngraben. "The accountant," says Tolstoy, "a stout, full-faced man, looked around him with a naïve smile of satisfaction and presented a strange appearance among the hussars, Cossacks and adjutants in his camlet coat, as he jolted on his horse with a convoy officer's saddle" (W&P, 191). There is absolutely no reason for this accountant to be present at the scene, so why is he there? One might say the reason is comic relief, or color, but there is more to it than that. After all, this man is just as conspicuous as and physically similar to Pierre at the Battle of Borodino, who stumbled around among the dying soldiers in his white coat and big green hat. These two figures, in their grotesque contrast to their surroundings, do establish a link of thematic relevance, of ironic perspective, between the two battles. We never learn what the accountant reaped from his experience, but we do know that for Pierre Borodino was a crucial turning point; yet, as we see him realize what he has learned, we also understand that the same potential existed for the accountant at Schöngraben, that is, truth appears in many modulations.

Another instance, from the very beginning of the novel, involves Prince Vassily's "bald, scented, and shining head" being "presented" to Madame Sherer as he kisses her hand; this image comes back to us as an absurdly comical memory when in his dream Pierre sees the shining globe covered with droplets of water (*W&P*, 1181), a symbol from which Pierre learns that God is in the midst of everything and that all of us try to reflect God to the fullest extent possible. Prince Vassily, of course, was lying about everything to his hostess with great skill and charm. There are so many of such correspondences and recurrences, ironic or somber, emerging again and again as we delve more deeply into the text, that it almost seems as though every last detail must have a counterpart somewhere else in the text.

As signifiers, the focal-point objects can also be compared to Tolstoy's mechanical metaphors, such as the stripped screw that turns idly in Pierre's mind when he is at his wit's end, the spinning mill of moving guests supervised by Madame Sherer at her soirée, or the fantastically huge clock mechanism that begins to move the armies inexorably toward the Battle of Austerlitz. The extended beehive metaphor describing the evacuation of Moscow before the arrival of Napoleon's armies is a biological version of the same metaphorical constructs. The difference, of course, is that the beehives and spinning mills don't actually exist as objects in the novel, as compared to the sofa and other such objects. What is real in the novel and imaginary in the narrator's mind thus function on the same plane of signification. Hence, all dimensions of the text turn toward the metaphorical.

In further examining his use of the sofa, we see that Tolstoy is careful not to order all the events around the exact same piece of furniture, but that he modulates the symbol from a sofa in one place to a couch in another, or again, to a movable field bed, thereby reinforcing the message in a given situation through its relation to other symbols. This device expands the base of situational relevance, and indeed, validates the device itself, because if any such situational sign is isolated, it will not "rhyme" and will lose it relevance to the general design.

In the second category of narrational isotopes, Tolstoy expands the rhyming principle to the systematic use of what could be called markers—repeated references in the text to body parts, objects, situations, and even feelings and trains of thought. The most evident of these markers are recurrences in the physical details of a person's description, such as Lise's upper lip, Hélène's naked shoulders and bosom, Pierre's enormous bulk, Prince Vassily's bald pate and his habit of pulling down the other person's hand when shaking hands, Mary Bolkonsky's luminous eyes and heavy tread, Kutuzov's obese drowsiness, Karataev's good-hearted roundness, Napoleon's twitching calf, and so on. Many critics have commented on this famous Tolstoyan device. In effect, a physical detail, repeated in constantly changing situations, ceases to be merely a personal trait and becomes a process, an ongoing relationship between a person and the surrounding world, in which that person's image is being continually modified, together with the expanding universe of the novel itself.

R. F. Christian, among others, has drawn our attention to a slightly different kind of recurrence, namely, that of situations, actions, thoughts, and feelings that seem to map out the forthcoming sets of events in the novel, thus providing it with a cohesive shape. This recurrence belongs to the third type of narrative isotope. Christian cites among his examples Nikolay Rostov's reaction to the news of Natasha's engagement to Andrey, namely, his belief "that the marriage will not take place" (Christian, 133); Nikolay's premonition reveals itself later to be part of Tolstoy's design for future events, and at which the author is already hinting. We could add another indication that the marriage will not take place. In chapter 7 Nastasya Ivanovna, the male clown in woman's dress, says that Natasha's children will be "fleas, crickets, grasshoppers" (*W&P*, 571), that is, nobody. Christian rightly notes that "the fact that clues to the outcome of an eventual situation or relationship are sometimes given at a very early stage—long before that situation or relationship has begun to be determined—may be regarded as another link in the chain which holds the novel together" (Christian, 133).

Still another type of recurrence pertains to several series of repeating elements, each of them quite independent of one another, related to different characters, and separated in place and time, but which, in the totality of the series, functions to establish some structurally significant common thematic statement. There are, for instance, the recurrences connected with peoples' legs and feet. In Book 3, while awaiting the visit of Prince Vassily and his son, Kuragin, Prince Bolkonsky is already out of temper because young Kuragin threatens to take away the prince's daughter in marriage. Tikhon, the servant, says to the house architect: "Do you hear how he's walking? . . . Stepping flat on his heels—we know what that means" (*W&P*, 232). Having already been introduced to Kuragin, the reader can well sympathize with Bolkonsky's anger, though not with his possessive, cruel love for Mary. Irony reigns when we remember that Mary always walks with a heavy tread; thus, the loving, humble, oppressed daughter steps just like the loving, proud, angry father, and we wonder how similar father and daughter really are.

When Vassily and his son Anatoly Kuragin arrive in Bald Hills, we learn from the maid that Vassily, the father, dragged himself up the stairs with difficulty while young and handsome Anatoly "followed him like an eagle, three steps at a time" (*W&P*, 235). Just a little later young Kuragin also proves quite adept at playing footsie under the clavichord with Mary's companion, Mademoiselle Bourienne, while the two appear to be gazing admiringly at Mary, who is playing her favorite piece of music for them. At this point the markers "feet" and "music," with their attendant notions of "true feeling" and "deceit," come together as the governing devices that convey various levels of meaning in many situations in the novel. For instance, we see Natasha, who is frustrated by Andrey's absence and must endure the time of separation forced upon her and Andrey by old Bolkonsky, recovering a sense of self with a few musical phrases and firm steps on the floor: "'Things are nice as it is,' she said to herself, and she began walking up and down the room, not stepping simply on the resounding parquet but treading with each step from the heel to the toe (she had on a new and favorite pair of shoes) and listening to the regular tap of the heel and creak of the toe as gladly as she had to the sounds of her own voice" (*W&P*, 523).

An ominous corollary to Natasha's resolute steps is provided by Andrey in the field at Borodino. Standing in reserve under artillery fire, he "walked along the meadow, dragging his feet, rustling the grass, and gazing at the dust that covered his boots; now he took big strides trying to keep to the footprints left on the meadow by the mowers, then he counted his steps, calculating how often he must walk from one strip to another to walk a mile, then he stripped the flowers from the wormwood that grew along a boundary rut, rubbed them in his palms, and smelled their pungent, sweetly bitter scent" (*W&P*, 903). All this close attention to how Andrey walked, superfluous in a description not meant to establish other linkages, brings to memory Natasha sitting and watching the dancer Duport jumping up and down on his fat legs at the opera, a glittering affair during which Natasha succumbs to the vicious charms of the fleet-footed Kuragin. It is, of course, only poetic justice that we see Kuragin moaning in terror and despair, having just lost his leg in the battle. Andrey pities and forgives him, yet the marker reappears: Andrey's thighbone is removed by the battlefield surgeon. This incident brings us back to Smolensk and the beginning of Napoleon's campaign, at which time a shopkeeper woman was wounded in the thigh as Andrey watched. We might even remember Napoleon's twitching calf just before the Battle of Borodino. The foot marker also leads us to the hunting party, where Natasha dances a Russian folk dance wondrously well, and earlier, to the ball, where her father pleases everybody with his "Daniel Cooper" (a figure of the *anglaise* [see *W&P*, 72]), as well as to many other situations, large and small, all having to do with love and death, falsehood, and retribution in the lives of the main fictional characters.[3]

Legs and feet are convenient and effective choices for object-metaphors in a novel full of movement and action, but they do not have a literary tradition of established associations that would in themselves define their significance in a narrative. Nonetheless, Tolstoy's other recurrent device, doors and candles, does bring with it literary and popular conventions associated with birth and death. Since these metaphors, or isotopes, establish a level of meaning pertaining to these two main events in our lives, Tolstoy extends them across most of the novel, placing them in action situations in the presence of other devices and various characters.

In Book 3 the Rostovs are at home while their son Nikolay is at the front at Austerlitz. Having recovered from his injury—a wrist sprained falling from his horse—Nikolay writes a letter to his family about it. Old Count Rostov is worried about how to tell the news to his wife without throwing her into panic. Fortunately, Anna Mikhailovna, the busybody mother of Boris Drubetskoy, is there and undertakes to break the news to the countess gently. She goes to the countess's room, closes the door, and the count, listening behind it, hears:

> Anna Mikhailovna's voice alone in a long speech, then a cry, then silence, then both voices together with glad intonations, and then footsteps. Anna Mikhailovna opened the door. Her face wore the proud expression of a surgeon who has just performed a difficult operation and admits the public to appreciate his skill.
> "It is done!" she said to the count. (*W&P*, 252–53)

In this scene the surgeon is a metaphor, but there is a real doctor in the tragic episode of Lise's death in childbirth. The scene takes place in Bald Hills, Andrey is absent and presumed dead, and Lise's labor is about to begin. The midwife comes, the doctor is still expected, and the huge sofa we noted before is brought into the bedroom. The candles are lit before the religious icons. "Suddenly, a gust of wind beat violently at the casement of the window . . . [and] set the damask curtain flapping and blew out the candle" (*W&P*, 351); Tolstoy makes a clear connection here between snuffed candles and death. Soon thereafter someone drives up the avenue, the wind again blows out the candles outside, and Andrey, covered with snow, comes in from the storm. Then the doctor comes, and Andrey hears "piteous, helpless animal moans" through the closed door. "Prince Andrew got up, went to the door, and tried to open it. Someone was holding it shut" (*W&P*, 353). The sound of a baby crying follows, and: "The door opened.

The doctor with his shirt sleeves tucked up, without a coat, pale and with a trembling jaw, came out of the room. Prince Andrew turned to him, but the doctor gave him a bewildered look and passed by without a word" (*W&P*, 353).

Lise is dead. From our reader's distance we can now see that for Countess Rostova, the news that Nikolay is not seriously hurt amounts to something like the second birth of her son. Thus the metaphor's basic elements are established: doors, voices behind them, doctors, and the opening of these doors with joyful and terrible news of birth and death. The Rostova–Mikhailovna episode, of course, reads rather like a preliminary parody of Lise's death; in fact, the devices are the same, and the parody may well have been intentional, if we agree with Saul Morson that *War and Peace* is a highly parodic book.

At the birth of his child, Andrey tries to push open the closed door of the room in which Lise is delivering. The reverse happens at the threshold of his own death, during which he has a dream: The room he was in was full of people, all of whom eventually left,

> and a single question, that of the closed door, superseded all else. . . . He rose and went to the door to bolt and lock it. Everything depended on whether he was, or was not, in time to lock it. He went, and tried to hurry, but his legs refused to move and he knew he would not be in time to lock the door though he painfully strained all his powers. He was seized by an agonizing fear. And that fear was the fear of death. *It* stood behind the door. But just when he was clumsily creeping toward the door, that dreadful something on the other side was already pressing against it and forcing its way in. Something not human—death—was breaking in through that door and had to be kept out. He seized the door, making a final effort to hold it back—to lock it was not longer possible—but his efforts were weak and clumsy and the door, pushed from behind by that terror, opened and closed again.
>
> Once again *it* pushed from outside. His last superhuman efforts were vain and both halves of the door noiselessly opened. *It* entered, and it was *death*, and Prince Andrey died.
>
> But at the instant he died, Prince Andrew remembered that he was asleep, and at the very instant he died, having made an effort, he awoke. (*W&P*, 1090)

We can see the inversion: In the first instance Andrey tries to push open the closed door (as if he himself were the Death of his dream, the messenger of death for his wife!), and in the second he tries to keep the door shut, for behind it there is his own death and life (portrayed as an awakening). This mirror image attends the two fatal events and materializes in its implications the entire principle of Tolstoy's thoughts on life and death.

The image of a candle is used by Tolstoy at Lise's death in such a way that it almost becomes a melodramatic stage device. This device extends in a similar theatrical manner to the description of Pierre's induction into the Masonic order. This time it is a lamp inside a human skull, Tolstoy adds, "with its cavities and teeth."[4] A candle is also present when Andrey lies in his delirium in Mytishchi, and when his son Nikolay is ill (*W&P*, 402), and in several other contextually comparable places in the novel. Under the general notion of "light shining in darkness," this image emanates both mystery and clarity in relation to death. One of the most lucid, and in its way most terrible moments of clarity comes to Andrey around the image of a lamp just before the Battle of Borodino. He has received and given his orders, there is nothing more to do, and in this empty moment, "his thoughts—the simplest, clearest, and therefore most terrible thoughts—would give him no peace."[5] Death presents itself to him in its simplest aspect—in relation to himself and nothing else: "And from the height of this perception all that had previously tormented and preoccupied him suddenly became illumined by a cold white light without shadows, without perspective, and without distinction of outline. All life appeared to him like magic-lantern pictures at which he had long been gazing by artificial light through a glass. Now he suddenly saw those badly daubed pictures in clear daylight and without a glass" (*W&P*, 858).

Seeing these figures "in the cold white daylight of his clear perception of death," Andrey knows how crude they are; all those notions of glory, love of fatherland, and the good of society to which he previously had assigned so much value seem worthless to him now. This scene is one more instance of Tolstoy's device of "making strange," only this time it is death itself that makes up the rules of the game, and these rules define all our ideas about the meaning of life, or its irrelevance.

Finally, the image of the door serves to reopen a relationship between Pierre and Natasha, a door that will lead to their marriage. The harbinger of death now becomes the sign of life: "But at that moment Princes Mary said, 'Natasha!' And with difficulty, effort and stress, like the opening of a door grown rusty on its hinges, a smile appeared on the face with the attentive eyes, and from that opening door came a breath of fragrance which suffused Pierre with a happiness he had long forgotten and of which he had not even been thinking—especially at that moment. When she smiled doubt was no longer possible, it was Natasha and he loved her" (*W&P*, 1235). The room in which they meet is lit by just one candle, and Natasha is in black. Death and life are again copresent at this decisive moment, just as in the past.

Some events in the novel can be thought of as isotopic recurrences because between them they create a balanced entity with its own meaning, a sort of text. They may occur simultaneously but be separated by space, or they may be independent of time and space parameters, but together they contain some particular significance for the story. Sherer's party and Bagration's battle of Schöngraben are a case in point. When read in conjunction with each other, like a single text, these events seem to create a statement, perhaps that the meaningless stupidity of the high and mighty of the world corresponds directly to the horrors and stupidities of the slaughter in war. Thus, on the plane of historical argument, the events become the equivalent of each other. Moreover, the ritual dance of life in Sherer's ballroom weaves a pattern of lies (that is, social proprieties) to hide the knowledge of death lurking below the cobweb of artificial human relationships; this event is counterbalanced with the death of Pierre's father, which occurs simultaneously. Similarly, the tsar's party in Vilnius coincides with the sudden news of Napoleon's invasion. Considering that this juxtaposition actually took place in history, we might say that life itself collaborated with Tolstoy's design.

Another recurrence, a trivial event, brackets the entire Battle of Austerlitz. Before the battle, at the moment when Andrey is dreaming of his upcoming military exploits and frankly admits to himself his thirst for glory, he hears the voice of Kutuzov's coachman teasing the general's old cook:

> "Tit, I say, Tit!"
> "Well?" returned the old man.
> "Go, Tit, thresh a bit!" said the wag.
> "Oh, go to the devil!" called out a voice, drowned by the laughter of the orderlies and servants. (W&P, 284)

As if in refrain to this silly joke, Andrey thinks to himself: "All the same, I love and value nothing but triumph over them all, I value this mystic power and glory that is floating here above me in this mist!" For the moment, we may stop here and remember the role of mist in "The Cossacks" and in *War and Peace* as a symbol of illusions. After the battle, when the Russian troops are utterly defeated and subjected to a wholesale slaughter by the French, we hear again:

> "Tit, I say, Tit!" said the groom.
> "What?" answered the old man absent-mindedly.
> "Go, Tit, thresh a bit!"
> "Oh, you fool!" said the old man, spitting angrily. Some time passed in silence, and then the same joke was repeated. (W&P, 310)

The phrase in Russian is *"Tit, stupay molotit',"* with *molotit'*—to thresh—being known as a metaphor in literature for the mass killing and mangling of the Russian troops on the battlefield. The Soviet scholar V. Ermilov likens this passage to the scenes of comic relief in Shakespeare, and then interprets it to mean that the Russian people, along with their representative, General Kutuzov, did not wish to go to this particular "threshing," having nothing but contempt for this upper-class war.[6] We could add that this phrase frames the entire battle between Andrey's illusions of glory and the realities of total defeat, the latter of which includes Andrey's own understanding, as he lies wounded looking at the sky, of how worthless the dream of glory is. There also may be a further connection: In Russian literature the use of the agricultural metaphor of threshing to describe a bloody battle goes back to the famous twelfth-century epic *Lay of the Host of Igor'*, which describes another historic defeat of the Russian forces by the Polovtsians.[7] Here Tolstoy again may be using the device of privileged information shared only with the reader, because the two humble Russian folk participating in the lame joke could not have the faintest awareness of the ancient tale.

A recurring image throughout the novel involves a wide-open, wild glance, like that of a cornered animal. Indeed, its first use does involve an animal—the wolf captured in the hunt at Otradnoe, in Book 7: "The huntsmen . . . all came to look at the wolf, which, with her broad-browed head hanging down and the bitten stick between her jaws, gazed with great glassy eyes at this crowd of men and dogs surrounding her. When she was touched, she jerked her bound legs and looked wildly yet simply at everybody" (*W&P*, 553). Then, in Book 8, we see Natasha, who had so joyfully participated in the hunt, sitting in a corner, with Pierre and Marya Dmitrievna Akhrosimova, the plainspoken "terrible dragon." Natasha's plan to elope with Kuragin has just been thwarted, and Pierre has come to tell her that Kuragin could not have taken her for a wife because he was already married. Natasha, cornered, "looked from one to the other as a wounded animal looks at the approaching dogs and sportsmen" (*W&P*, 654). There is, of course, no possible ordinary connection between the hunt and this scene, but Tolstoy's deliberate choice of comparing Natasha with a hunted animal establishes an image contact between the two scenes and thus creates a semantic plane upon which we can see the utter despair Natasha has been thrown into by her misadventure with the "sportsman" Kuragin. Pierre himself, when confronted by Hélène after his duel with Dolokhov, has a similar look: "Pierre looked at her timidly over his spectacles, and like a hare surrounded by hounds who lays back her ears and continues to crouch motionless before her enemies, he tried to continue reading" (*W&P*, 344). The image of the enormous Pierre crouching like a rabbit with his ears pulled back makes him look ridiculous (and, by design, Pierre often looks ridiculous in the novel). But during the same scene the terrible and monstrous force in him rises up to lift and smash a huge marble slab, making the panicky Hélène run away.[8]

Finally, we see these eyes again in Moscow, at the execution of Russian "incendiaries" in Book 11: "The convicts stopped when they reached the post and, while sacks were being brought, looked dumbly around as a wounded beast looks at an approaching huntsman" (*W&P*, 1069). A little later, these eyes reappear in the face of a young factory lad about to be shot. His execution involves the recurrence of another image, first used at Pierre's Masonic initiation:

> The lad was unable to walk. They dragged him along, holding him up under the arms, and he screamed. When they got him to the post, he grew quiet, as if he suddenly understood something. Whether he understood that screaming was useless or whether he thought it incredible that men should kill him, at any rate he took his stand at the post, waiting to be blindfolded like the others, and like a wounded animal looked around him with glittering eyes. . . . When they began to blindfold him he himself adjusted the knot which hurt the back of his head. (*W&P*, 1070)

We may recall the scene in which Willarski blindfolds Pierre during the Masonic initiation ritual: "having taken a kerchief from the cupboard, Willarski bound Pierre's eyes with it and tied it in a knot behind, catching some hairs painfully in the knot" (*W&P*, 386). The irony of this juxtaposition comes into full force when we remember that one of the things required of Pierre for his initiation into the Freemasons was the love of death—precisely the Masonic virtue he could never manage to acquire. The execution of the boy is firmly branded as a crime: "They [the French] all plainly and certainly knew that they were criminals who must hide the traces of their guilt as quickly as possible" (*W&P*, 1071). The recurrent image of pulled hair marks the young factory lad's transition to death as well as Pierre's transition to a very different world of thought. Of course, the Masonic hope for peace, harmony, and eternal light is cruelly mocked by the comparison. After all, we must not forget that the French Tolstoy describes were the children of their revolution, children of a reason with its roots in the Encyclopedists.

The irony works backwards as well, so that we may consider a "supertext" that is suggested by these and other recurrences in the novel. Every occurrence of the wild eyes image signals an act of violence against nature, perpetrated by people who consider hunting to be a merry sport; against Natasha's soul, perpetrated by Kuragin and Dolokhov; and against the sacred gift of life itself. In some ultimate sense, all these acts are crimes against nature, humankind, and God. Taken together they signify the true nature of all violence, especially that of this enormous Napoleonic War that fell upon Russia. Thus an image, a descriptive technique, exists in that supertext as a statement of values—specifically, that image is pacifism, which characterized all of Tolstoy's later teachings.

Finally, we might mention another small set of recurring images with a supertext of its own. It has to do with prayer. In Book 9 the scene is set at a special church service in Moscow offered for the deliverance of the country from the invaders. "The priest," writes Tolstoy, "came out with his purple velvet biretta on his head, adjusted his hair, and knelt down with an effort. Everybody followed his example and they looked at one another in surprise" (*W&P*, 734). The scene then shifts to Borodino just before the battle, at the final prayers before the icon of the Holy Mother of God of Smolensk[9]: "When the service was over, Kutuzov stepped up to the icon, sank heavily to his knees, bowed to the ground, and for a long time tried vainly to rise, but could not do so on account of his weakness and weight. His white head twitched with the effort. At last he rose, kissed the icon as a child does with naïvely pouting lips, and again bowed till he touched the ground with his hand" (*W&P*, 852). In between these two temporal points stands Natasha, who is at the same church service at which the priest said his prayer: "She felt in her heart a devout and tremulous awe at the thought of the punishment that overtakes men for their sins, and especially of her own sins, and she prayed to God to forgive them all, and her too, and to give them all, and her too, peace and happiness. And it seemed to her that God heard her prayer" (*W&P*, 736).

What unites these three points is affliction and prayer on the eve of a momentous event that will turn around the course of the war and bring about Russia's resurrection. All three characters are carrying a heavy burden: The priest is bent by the burden of both the desecration of his land and the responsibility before God to ask for deliverance; Kutuzov is bent by his awesome responsibility for defending the violated land, and Natasha bears the burden of her own recent desecration in the affair with Kuragin as she prays for forgiveness for her own sins and the sins of everyone in the world. The weight of the burdens of the first two characters is symbolized by the difficulty with which they kneel and get up. As we watch Kutuzov struggling to rise, we may be torn in our feelings between the ridiculous and the sublime. The ridiculous element is present in the knowledge that the reason for Kutuzov's difficulty is simply that he is old and fat; as such, his action has no meaning just prior to such a terrible battle. The sublime element surfaces when, remembering the priest's prayer, we may feel we are watching the entire land struggling to rise from its affliction under the French, an act that is extremely difficult indeed, and one that Kutuzov might rightly personify at the moment. Natasha, too, may become symbolic: Innocent and violated, she is the Russian land, and God will hear her prayer. The reason He will do so may also reveal the secret of Russia's strength, namely, the righteousness of Russia's people, as shown through Natasha, who "could not pray that her enemies might be trampled under foot when but a few minutes before she had been wishing she had more of them that she might pray for them. But neither could she doubt the righteousness of the prayer that was being read on bended knees" (W&P, 736). Praying for one's enemies in the hour of affliction—this is actually what elevates Natasha to the level of a symbol of Russia's resurrection. On this symbolic level, images of prayer connect with and balance the recurrent images of violence, again through the transitional symbol of Natasha, who is a part of both sequences.

There are quite a few other, similar chains of recurrences in the novel, but they approach one general point. Recurrences of the same element in different contexts create new yet related sets of meanings, thus becoming enriched themselves and, through mutual associations, creating more levels of meaning through the varying contexts related to them. By permitting comparison and counterpoint, these recurrences function like metaphors. Earlier we analyzed narrative or situational rhymes in the novel, and the extended metaphors that characterized some of them. All such terms come from the genre of poetry, as does the term *recurrences*. In a very real sense, to talk about *War and Peace* is to talk about a kind of poetry, which some have called epic. It is also important to perceive that the world created by all these recurrences is in itself a supertext with a reality of its own. This world permits us new perceptions, and thus the novel builds its own space by creating a figurative simultaneity in that space. Earlier we explored the idea of time acquiring body and substance to become history; here we have an ultimate algorithm, a configuration of necessities, which acquires the materialization and dynamics of peoples' experiences and relationships in order to become that which, together with time, shapes both fiction and history. There seems to be an unnamed dimension in the novel in which forces that constitute the deepest essence of reality turn and move according to laws of their own while the world we can see configures itself in accordance with the movements of these mysterious forces.

8

Dynamics and Building Blocks

Strings of related images, objects, or places, which serve as focal points that bring together disparate events in *War and Peace*, as well as "situation rhymes" and isotopes, which mark the ideological and emotional terrain, contribute to a sense of unity in the novel. These ties, which often become visible only upon close reading, may also seem too fragile to hold such a colossus together. Yet their network may not be so densely woven after all. There may be free spaces, that is, large sequences of events, movements across wide distances, or even endless meandering rivulets of people's daily comings and goings, that do not require systems of echoes and recurrences to establish a valid function for them in the structure of the novel. Yet we do need some general sense of structure, something beyond given particulars, if we are to appeal Henry James's verdict that *War and Peace* is a "loose and baggy monster."

Structure begins with an overall concept, a basic idea. From Tolstoy's own testimony, we can discern that he meant to start something large and free-flowing, something that would be "majestic, deep and many-sided" in content, as Tolstoy wrote in the first draft of his introduction to the novel (*W&P*, 1363), and that did not fit easily under the designation of novel. Tolstoy's intent would imply, first, freedom from the criteria of genre definitions and, second, freedom from the restrictions of what conventional genres concern themselves with, such as the story of a romance, a realistic tale of everyday life, a traditional historical novel, or even, as Tolstoy himself put it, freedom from the need "to solve a question irrefutably" (letter to P. D. Boborykin [see *W&P*, 1359]), that is, make a convincing statement on some social concern. All these elements, even the last, do exist within the framework of *War and Peace*, but the text also encompasses something larger than the sum of its relationships.

The simplest model of the novel's structure can be derived from its very title: war and peace. These two opposing conditions suggest a binary principle at work in the entire text. On a broad scale, Tolstoy presents Russia opposed to France, the Russian ruling classes opposed to the Russian people as a whole, and, in the conduct of war, the argumentative theoreticians, mostly Germans or other foreigners, versus the inarticulate but truly strong Russian folk. This notion of folk includes some Russian generals—Kutuzov (who makes do with two words, "time" and "patience," when describing how he hopes to win the war); Dokhturov, a humble, competent Russian; the Armenian Bagration; such officers and soldiers as Timokhin and Tushin; and the quintessential Russian spirit, round and smelly Karataev.[1] Another basic opposition—historical versus invented characters—brings us to the plane of fictional conflicts and resolutions taking place under the avalanche of history. There the opposition involves that "nest of vipers" the Kuragins, including father, daughter Hélène, and sons Anatoly and Ippolit, versus the good Rostovs and the troubled Bolkonskys. During the ball at which Natasha and Andrey fall in love, Tolstoy visually contrasts her with Hélène in a way that goes counter to established clichés in romantic literature, namely, the stupid and evil Hélène is golden blond and radiant, while the lovable Natasha is dark-haired and gawky. In the same way, Prince Vassily, a member of the highest societal circles, lacks any principles or moral sense whatsoever, and is a perfect contrast to Prince Bolkonsky, a man of deep humanity who is nonetheless frozen stiff with pride and principle. Tolstoy presents German and Russian versions of handsome, vain, stupid and self-worshipping officers: Berg and Drubetskoy. In the same way, the joyful goings-on at "uncle's" after the hunt are counterpointed by the dancing, skinny Natasha and the laughing, fat Anisya. The main events of the plot are set off in binary sets. Under the rubric of war, Andrey is seriously wounded at Austerlitz, Russia's greatest defeat, and mortally so at its greatest victory, Borodino; under peace, his great romantic love, Natasha, becomes the loving wife of his best friend, Pierre. Present-day English readers are spared the very long passages in French spoken by Tolstoy's aristocrats.[2] These passages are also an intrusion into the Russian text, creating ironic echoes of the intrusion of French culture into Russian society and, finally, the intrusion of French military forces into Russian land. Thus one can think of *War and Peace* as binary work even in the linguistic sense. According to R. F. Christian, this binary balance is indeed the governing structural principle of the novel: "It seems to me that the principle of composition is to think of people and phenomena in terms of their opposites and then to contrive the juxtaposition and interaction of these opposites" (Christian, 124).

The binary principle permits alternations in the arrangements of the novel's parts: Scenes of peace are followed by ones of war, and with this progression comes a change of emphasis among the family chronicles, the lives and loves of the main fictional heroes, and the grand advance of history that radically changed those characters' fortunes. The critic Albert Cook, on the basis of his conviction that "the fifteen books and Epilogue of the novel are orchestrated into an almost contrapuntal order, war and peace being not . . . disorganized strands, but the basic alternation, each defining the other, of the plot's form" (*W&P*, 1400), carefully follows those parts, maintaining that each of them sustains a particular mood and perception of both individual existence and history. Cook's point is not really shaken by the fact that the books in the Norton edition of the novel do not alternate exactly. Book 1 occurs in peacetime, with Andrey going off to war just at the section's very end. All of Book 2 takes place at war. Book 3 is mixed, beginning with another soirée at Sherer's, and ending with Andrey's wound at Austerlitz. Book 4 details a time of peace, as does Book 5, except at its end, when it relates Nikolay Rostov's and Denisov's misadventures at the front, and the peace of Tilsit. Book 6 takes place in peacetime, as does Book 7, in which Nikolay returns to his regiment. Book 8 is set in peacetime, Book 9 describes war, and Book 10 details peace in its first half, with war as a strong background presence that crashes onto the scene with the full fury of Borodino in the book's second half. Book 11 concerns neither peace nor war, but the aftermath of Napoleon's completed march to Moscow, in which Pierre's troubles and capture are detailed. Book 12 describes peace; it begins with another soirée at Sherer's and ends, ironically, with Andrey's death. Such arrangement in itself acquires message attributes, for it confronts the topic of death with the notion of the meaningless life of high society. Books 13 and 14 are all about war, while Book 15 mixes war and peace; then follow the two epilogues. Originally this material was divided into six volumes (Aylmer Maude did not provide such a division), but, as Ralph Matlaw has carefully noted, in 1873 Tolstoy reorganized the text into four volumes, achieving greater thematic and structural unity (*W&P*, 1416–23).

A set of alternations that reveals some overall design can be perceived as a mosaic. Boris Eikhenbaum proposes the notion of the novel being built on the principle of a mosaic, with the narrative tied together by means of juxtaposed blocks of settings and actions that may be perceived as equivalents of one another. Thus, according to Eikhenbaum, Tolstoy put together in his novel a montage of ideas about history that were gleaned from various external sources (Eikhenbaum II, 338). Actually, Tolstoy extended this procedure to some segments in the action of the novel, such as the execution of Vereschchagin, in Book II, taken from historical sources and then modified for the novel. Finally, as we noted previously, the very fact that the novel first came out in installments contributes a good deal to the impression of its being composed in blocks, which sometimes grind against one another.

As we think of binary contrasts and of pieces of the mosaic intruding upon each other, the face of the novel that emerges seems wounded, jagged, and torn by contrasts. Yet, when we return to our initial reading of the novel, it does not seem to be a work at war with itself. Evidently, there is yet another unifying principle that is stronger than any contrasting structures. We could think of it in terms of a certain energy. Every encounter of different elements, be they binary opposites of each other or construction blocks, creates a relationship, a certain tension that can generate new meanings or resolve the conflicts of previous perceptions. Finding these meanings can make for delightful reading. The dynamics of action, the thrust and force that one can feel in the novel as a whole, leads to a more organic, developmental view.

One such view, proposed by Boris Eikhenbaum, is that, in opposition to the ideas of social progress and a civilization based on rationality, Tolstoy originally meant to write a story asserting the values of ordinary family life as contrasted with the public values proclaimed by history. The work could then be seen as passing through wider and wider spheres of reference until its very nature began to change from an idyll to an epic. The heightened style necessary for an epic was provided in the general expository passages conveying Tolstoy's thoughts on history, determinism, and freedom of will, the sources of power, and so on. These passages had the effect of "Homeric digressions" (Eikhenbaum II, 376). The problem is, of course, that the digressions in *The Iliad*, such as the one about Achilles' shield, are not contemplative, but descriptive.

This idea of progression from family to history to epos, with the attendant rise in the level of language, and with increasing clarity of Tolstoy's purpose, is disputed by some scholars, such as R. F. Christian, who rejects the idea that there was an evolution toward the epic as the writing of *War and Peace* progressed: "All these ingredients are alluded to in one form or another in the earliest plans and drafts of the novel and make nonsense of the suggestion that they—or some of them—were necessitated by a later elevation of genre" (Christian, 121). Christian also states that Tolstoy never thought of his contemplative digressions as "Homeric elements" (Christian, 13). Instead, Christian believes that they merely distract from both the unity of action in and the genre of the book.

Epic or not, the digressions do represent in the overall structure of the text one of its three basic aspects; the other two are historical events and fictional lives. It may be argued that such disparate modes are generally not found together in a well-written novel because they are not compatible: History deals with facts that already have occurred, fiction speaks of what never was, and expository prose is a metalanguage about both. Nonetheless, Gary Morson draws our attention to Victor Shklovsky's observation that "the tendency to mix fiction and nonfiction, romance and scholarship, novel and history, in a single work" was a distinct Russian tradition in the nineteenth century, and indeed, as much could be said of the eighteenth as well.[3]

The reason *War and Peace* does work as a unified text lies in the dynamics of how these main elements are spliced together to make a single strong thread. We may notice, for instance, that the opening parts of the novel do not really provide enough momentum to carry the weight of private lives. They seem to sink back into irrelevance or failure, as when Andrey comes back from the ball to his unloved wife, a conflict in which there is not enough drama to produce further action. Similarly, Pierre goes to a drunken party, where Dolokhov's stupid act of bravado—drinking an entire bottle of rum while sitting precariously on a third-floor windowsill with his back to the yard below—seems like a parody of heroic deeds. This scene cuts off any chance for any exciting challenge or quests in Pierre's future, especially when we see that his heroic role model, his lionlike father, dies at the very outset of the novel. The Rostovs, it would seem, can do no more than eat, drink, and dance; a vivacious wisp of a girl like Natasha has no power upon which to build a large novel; nor can Hélène's face launch any ships. There is nothing in the initial setting of the book to suggest strong forward motion.

Real action, both in the private and the historical sphere, begins only after the narrativity of these fictional lives—their ability to act out a story—is ignited by the historical event of Napoleon's invasion. This invasion also provides an opportunity for a ponderous philosophical discourse about the meaning of events. Thus arises the need to develop those private lives in a constant relationship with huge outside forces in order to show the reader how the fictional characters' responses to events prove the rightness of the proposed philosophy. The novel then becomes truth in action.

Therefore, perhaps the basic thread uniting all aspects of *War and Peace* is the interplay of individual and collective human experience. In Tolstoy's works, individuals carried by the flow of history retain their personal identity, and the integrity of their perceptions is not shattered by events. In that sense, for them there really is no history, but only an immediate personal experience. It is thus that Pierre sees the beginning of the Battle of Borodino:

> *Puff!*—suddenly a round compact cloud of smoke was seen merging from violet into gray and milky white, and *boom!* came the report a second later.
> *Puff! puff!*—and two clouds arose pushing one another and blending together; and *boom! boom!* came the sound confirming what the eye had seen. (*W&P*, 881)

Pierre makes no comment that would be suitable to a historic personage, such as, "A great battle is about to begin," or "Europe's fate is being decided today." He does not intellectualize, but instead responds with his emotions: He "wished to be there with that smoke, those shining bayonets, that movement and all those sounds" (*W&P*, 881). If an author can sustain this mode of communicating history to the reader, a task at which Tolstoy succeeds, then history is real only as it is absorbed into the personal experience of the fictional characters, and because it becomes so real, it loses all abstract meaning. John Bayley understands this device as an "annexation of history" through oneself, in which the reader may think, "All things I feel were felt by people in the past," and, "Everything stems from and depends upon our own existence" (Bayley, 70).

The same principle also operates in small details, most of which are remembered from Tolstoy's own past, as attested by numerous commentators. In Tolstoy's childhood, for instance, the young ladies in the house "made cheeses" by twirling around in their long skirts and then suddenly dipping down to make the material balloon out. In *War and Peace* Sonya does precisely the same thing (*W&P*, 323), so that a playful moment from Tolstoy's early life becomes part of the intimate fictional setting occurring in 1812. Thus, in Tolstoy's mind, the personal becomes the only reality the past can possess, and as its fictional characters enter the past, they give existence to their time. This existence becomes the only substance there is, but it varies according to each character; hence, all time and place is relative to the individual.[4] Obviously, then, there are no such things as general laws of history that can explain the present and predict the future by solving just one overall equation. The characters' individual experiences, then, are both their immediate realities and the gist of Tolstoy's argument about history. As people move through the novel, like a stream of consciousness, time itself is being formed, acquiring body and shape, and in this sense, becoming history. All an author can do, then, is describe the relationships between one circumscribed universe and all others, the droplets of water in Pierre's dream. Stepping across the line from the historical to the philosophical-metaphysical dimension, all these relationships acquire the yearning to become one, to embody all. Of course, Tolstoy would never undertake to speak of one and all in his own voice, because in his hard-nosed world such terms are much too vague. They are useful only in the characters' fictional space as artistic devices, to help convey a human state of belief, as with the Masons, and a transcendent consciousness of death, as with Andrey. Yet, they do carry some sort of feeling that dwells in Tolstoy's own mind and heart, and demands realization. Victor Shklovsky speaks of Tolstoy's constant revising of the novel's structure, action, and human relationships in order to make them conform to an inner sense of what the core of life is all about (Shklovsky, 418). Albert Cook puts it this way: "Tolstoy is all the while individuating these people [the characters], analyzing attitudes of a specificity of bent and tempo which will recombine into deeper and deeper meaning" (*W&P*, 1401). *War and Peace* progresses not only in time and space, but also in depth. This experience envelops us both in our appreciation of the fictional plot and in our sense of the Tolstoyan version of developing history. Thus by the time Tolstoy gets around to discussing its laws and necessities, history is already imbued with our feelings about it, and our perception of it stems from the fictional aspect of the book.

Tolstoy's argument, while more or less implicit on every page and in all the thoughts and actions of his characters, is repeatedly articulated with ever-increasing strength and clarity in the author's own voice. This voice becomes more and more dominant in a constant interplay with all the other elements of the book, but most particularly with Andrey Bolkonsky's repeated perceptions and formulations, which are ironically counterpointed by an entire chain of Anna Pavlovna Sherer's soirées. There fools nonsensically discuss same subjects Andrey contemplates in his own mind as part of his inner journey toward death, and about which the author pontificates in expository prose. We should note the frequent juxtapositions of these soirées with fatal moments in the lives of Pierre and Andrey: In Book 1 Pierre's father dies, and books 3 and 12 mark Andrey's near-fatal wound at Austerlitz and his death. Against these shocks, the superficial and often foolish high society chatter continues as an ironic background throughout the text. At Sherer's first soirée we learn of the indifference of the high society drones to what goes on in real life, and of Pierre's and Andrey's enthusiasm for Napoleon. The next time Sherer is hostess there is not much theoretical discussion, but Prince Vassily, by his unconscious machinations to gain power over Pierre and advance his own position, demonstrates Tolstoy's argument that what actually occurs in history is a product of unpredictable events rather than deliberate planning by the mighty ones of this world. Another soirée takes place in Book 5, where the mindless Boris Drubetskoy becomes the "main dish" to be served up; given at the end of 1806, just at the time of Napoleon's crushing victory against the Prussians, the party's nonsense becomes the distant echo of reality. In Book 12 the soirée at Anna's, in addition to Andrey's death, becomes an ironic accompaniment to the death of Hélène and to the Russian victory at Borodino.

Critics have noted Tolstoy's attempts to put the embryonic forms of his own philosophy into his characters' mouths, be it with ironic or straightforward intent. E. E. Zaydenshnur notes that 14 of the 15 first drafts start the novel in a setting in which people of the same class but of different views converse about current events.[5] This enabled Tolstoy to start all the issues, and levels of their treatment, at once. Some versions begin with the author's own commentaries about what was said in Petersburg high society,[6] as in the thirteenth introductory variant, in which the role of rulers in the course of history is discussed from the author's viewpoint. This approach seems to indicate that Tolstoy's views of history did not emerge and develop as he was telling his tale, but were present early on, even as far back as the Yasnaya Polyana period, in which Tolstoy showed how irrelevant to schoolchildren were the elements that constitute the traditional record of history.

One might then accept the notion that Tolstoy's expository statements are constantly tied in with society's affairs—their passions, plots, and counterplots—so that the two compose a single meaningful entity instead of being incongruities artificially slapped together. There is also, then, a similar natural bond between private lives and historical events.

Another thread in the mixed fictional-historical texture of the novel, one that also contributes to the overall impression of meaningful unity, is the events in the mind and heart of Prince Andrey. We have already noted his perceptions at the war council in Drissa, as well as at the war council prior to the Battle of Austerlitz; in the latter Andrey still is dreaming about his own potential glory as a strategist of war, and in so doing he goes directly against the grain of Tolstoy's pacifism. No wonder, then, that Tolstoy punishes him by means of an enlightening physical wound at the battle. At Drissa Andrey was already capable of understanding that there is no science to war, a point Tolstoy strongly reiterates later in his own expository voice. At the end of Book 10, with the Battle of Borodino looming in the distance, it is again Andrey who understands something about Kutuzov that Tolstoy the author tries to convince us of in his own voice. Kutuzov, Andrey perceives, "despised knowledge and cleverness and knew of something else that would decide the matter—something independent of cleverness and knowledge" (*W&P*, 828). That was "something stronger and more important than his own will—the inevitable course of events" (*W&P*, 831). By the end of Book 10 Tolstoy hopes to leave us fully convinced, as Andrey is also convinced, that Kutuzov is right, and that the French shall ultimately "eat horseflesh" in defeat, as they actually did, both because Tolstoy the artist says they did and because history attests to it.

Andrey descends to deeper, more essential, as well as more emotional levels of Tolstoy's argument just before the Battle of Borodino.

First, he reaches the stage of understanding that is necessary in order to give us the key to Tolstoy's message. That key is death, that "cold white light" of his perception of death, death "without shadow, without perspective and without distinction of outline" (*W&P*, 858). A moment after his realization, when he speaks to Pierre of his resolve to win the battle, he does not speak the "patriotic" blather we might hear at Anna Sherer's soirées, but instead communicates a fathomless readiness to die when events come to such a pass, as they inevitably will, for the reasons Tolstoy has been explaining to us in his expository passages. We understand that, having now said everything on behalf of his author, Andrey must die, and so he does.

We first become aware of the author's expository voice at the start of Book 6, in which, as noted earlier, real life is contrasted with the counterfeit life of the various diplomats and mighty ones of the world. Before long Tolstoy tells us that kings are but history's slaves, and for our own part, we may remember Tsar Alexander weeping by the ditch after the Russian defeat at Austerlitz. At the beginning of Book 9, the authorial voice comes back to articulate this insight and lead us by way of it to an understanding of history's causalities: "To us . . . who are not historians and are not carried away by the process of research and can therefore regard the event with unclouded common sense, an incalculable number of causes present themselves. The deeper we delve in search of these causes the more of them we find; and each separate cause or whole series of causes appears to us equally valid in itself and equally false by its insignificance compared to the magnitude of events" (*W&P*, 668).

In Book 10 the voice tells us about the beginning of the campaign of 1812. There it makes a clear link with the fictional part by pointing out—almost in the manner of a literary critic, commenting upon his own fictional characters and placing them in the same series as historical characters—that one of the innumerable real reasons why the campaign began was because Nikolay Rostov "charged the French because he could not restrain his wish for a gallop across the field," exactly, we remember, as he could not restrain himself in the same way at the hunt back home in Otradnoe. We should add that this link establishes the basis for a long-standing suspicion—that the hunting scene is an extended metaphor for the events that will occur at the end of 1812. Napoleon's threat looms in the background, and in the shadow of that threat we are shown the deep qualities of Russian strength—the joy of the hunt, Natasha dancing, the unfathomable simplicity of rural life—which will be the source of Russian victory, of the spirit Andrey spoke of before the Battle of Borodino. The senselessness and inevitability of that battle are explained in the author's elaborate set of remarks in Book 10, in which Tolstoy spends a great deal of time showing us how wrong the historians were about everything. This argument may not be on the same abstract level as the one Tolstoy ultimately develops, for it is more a polemical commentary about particulars, but it does support the entire structure of his thought.

In Book 11, by way of introduction to Kutuzov's fateful decision to retreat from Moscow, the expository voice turns to the calculus of infinitely small magnitudes to explain why history cannot be segmented in order to search for its laws. Tolstoy argues that any segmentation will lead only to absurdities, as with the ancient Greek paradox of Achilles, who, no matter how swift, could never overtake the turtle, for his route could be measured in individual segments ad infinitum, and still there would remain a distance to be covered. In terms of the war, this metaphor suggests that Kutuzov's decision has in a real sense never actually been made at the end of any of its segments, just as Tolstoy says in another place (*W&P*, 918) that a general never deals with the *beginning* of any action, nor, by implication, does anyone else. In terms of ordinary life at peace, the process of living resembles an infinite calculus of imperceptible moments.[7]

From this argument follows a different way of reading the text. For instance, the inevitability of Pierre's loving Natasha follows from the fact that we cannot point to any precise moment during which this love began. What has no beginning was always there, and any markers in the text that make us realize that the two are falling in love only indicate what already exists. Similarly, considering that as we are born, we are also already dying, there can be no meaningful separate moment called death. This notion leads to the rather chilling insight that Andrey, in view of the things that happen to him, and with regard to his particular way of perceiving life, exemplifies with the greatest clarity that life is a process of dying.

The next argument by Tolstoy in Book 11 is one in which he lambasts the nonsensical logic used to explain events, using such arguments as: "Whenever I look at my watch and its hands point to ten, I hear the bells of the neighboring church; but because the bells begin to ring when the hands of the clock reach ten, I have no right to assume that the movement of the bells is caused by the position of the hands of the watch" (*W&P*, 919); this exposition leads him right back to the idea, always present in the fictional part of the novel as well as in the description of historical events, that such absurdities are equivalent to thinking that kings and rulers make history. It is thus easy to understand what makes Bagration and Kutuzov such good generals in Tolstoy's view: They knew, or rather, it was in their nature to give orders on the battlefield that would do no more than affirm already accomplished facts. In the book this principle seamlessly extends from historical events to private lives. For instance, Pierre Bezukhov proposes to Hélène at the party only after the proposal already had happened, in essence—a sequence was leading in that direction, one dominated by Prince Vassily's machinations, Hélène's creaking corset and the nearness of her body, the atmosphere of expectation of the event among all present at the party, and so on. In fact, Pierre never actually does propose; instead, Prince Vassily walks into the room and congratulates him on the fait accompli.[8]

The authorial voice continues with ever-increasing presence in Book 14 and the first epilogue, and culminates in the second, in which the entire structure of Tolstoy's argument is laid out. The structure's two fundamental issues are power and free will, and the background for them both is the history of the Napoleonic Wars. Tolstoy's main question is: What causes the movements of nations? His answer is elaborate. The ancients claimed it was divinity working through its anointed men, the leaders of nations, whose activity was regarded as representing the activity of the whole nation. For the moderns the cause is the "existence of a known aim to which these nations and humanity at large are tending," that aim being "freedom, equality, enlightenment, progress, civilization, and culture" (*W&P*, 1326), at least as these things are understood in the "small northwestern corner of Europe" that pretends to represent the values of humankind. Tolstoy elucidates his argument by noting that modern historians say the power to strive for these aims comes from "the relation that exists between the expression of someone's will and the execution of that will by others" (*W&P*, 1317). Yet, what leaders do will not generate a force equal to that generated by nations as a whole: An exchange of diplomatic notes is not a reason for thousands of people to start murdering each other. Mere individuals talking among themselves do not cause history to happen, for history is a mass movement. Further, those who articulate the aims of society take the least part in the execution of those aims, and those who directly engage in action carry the least personal responsibility because the causes of their actions are limited to their personal perceptions.

Yet, any action goes back to the individual performing it, and by the same token, to the question of his or her free will. Here Tolstoy resolves the issue in a deliberate paradox. On the one hand, "If in a thousand years one man in a million could act freely, that is, as he chose, it is evident that one single free act of that man's in violation of the laws governing human action would destroy the possibility of the existence of any laws for the whole of humanity."[9] On the other hand, "All man's efforts, all his impulses to life, are only efforts to increase freedom" (*W&P*, 1338). A striking testimony to the tenacity and endurance of such a desire is Pierre Bezukhov. Imprisoned by the French, Pierre begins to understand the inviolable gift of freedom in his and any human soul, and laughs heartily at the thought that the French guard who would not let him pass may think that Pierre is not free: "'Ha-ha-ha!' laughed Pierre. And he said aloud to himself: 'The soldier did not let me pass. They took me and shut me up. They hold me captive. What, me? Me? My immortal soul? Ha-ha-ha! Ha-ha-ha!' . . . And he laughed till tears started to his eyes."[10]

What this voice creates is the impression of a finely woven network, a spiderweb of impressions, thoughts, and feelings that crisscrossed Tolstoy's consciousness throughout his life. The resolution to the question of free will comes in the form of a simile, not argument:

As we stand in the middle of the field, our perception tells us that sure-
ly the earth is flat; as we look at the globe, we know it is round. It is
not a question of which is true; truth resides in, or rather, truth is the
constantly shifting relationship between these two real perspectives.

This explanation may be why the construction of the world of
the novel as a system of perceptions is so important: "To understand,
observe, and draw conclusions, man must first of all be conscious of
himself as living" (*W&P*, 1336–37). If the novel's characters are to act
according to some rational or emotional logic the author has conceived for them, they will be but marionettes; if they act by what they
feel, they are free in each of their actions and determined in the entire
structure of the work. Ultimately, says Tolstoy, "freedom is the thing
examined. Inevitability is what examines. Freedom is the content.
Inevitability is the form" (*W&P*, 1346–47). In art, content changes
according to form. In the novel this change would create different
kinds of consciousness, as different kinds of freedom issue forth from
the way in which the author shapes his text. Thus the argument that all
the impulses of an individual are directed toward expanding his or her
freedom is so directly relevant to Pierre's globe with its expanding
droplets that this argument itself may appear as the continuation of the
image.

Yet the final issue is whether or not the expository segments of
the text can be regarded as integral to it. We may agree that the
actions of the heroes, large and small, and their perceptions, wide-
ranging or minute, can be seen as esthetic transformations of the ideas
of the argument, but can the argument itself be *art*? The answer might
be that the argument is at least rhetoric, the precursor of all art. The
second epilogue seems to be built on two principles—parable and reit-
eration. Describing how some historians claim that power causes
events, while others claim that events generate power, Tolstoy elucidates the issue by describing what the peasants, not knowing the cause
of rain, say about it. According to them, "the wind has blown away the
clouds," or, "the wind has brought the clouds" (*W&P*, 1319), wind
being the equivalent of power in an intellectual argument. Tolstoy's
point is that the peasants' notion of wind is as indefinite and empty as
the historians' notion of power. The idea that a force can generate

only events commensurate with it is illuminated by Tolstoy's description of ignorant peasants who think that the locomotive is moved by the devil, by the smoke that billows from the train, or by a German inside it. A historian who only holds to his or her own theory is like botanist who, having seen a plant reproducing by one process, says that all other processes we see are but deviations from the true theory. Meaningless historical arguments are "like a broom fixed in front of a locomotive to clear the snow from the rails in front" (*W&P*, 1334). This notion very much resembles Pierre's stripped screw and the other "mechanical metaphors" in the novel. Tolstoy's way of describing states of being is similar to his way of developing arguments about power and history.

All these hybrids of image and metaphor are developed in a ponderous, elephantine progression, with the points of argument and the images supporting them continually repeated, like the motifs in a Bruckner symphony, until one begins to sense that Tolstoy's chief anxiety is to making sure he has expressed himself exhaustively and lucidly, for fear that otherwise he might not be understood. This particular feeling aligns with Tolstoy's equally ponderous thoughts about the essence of art: If you conceive of an idea, have a feeling about it, and can convey it in such a way that everyone else will see the truth of that idea and get caught up in the same feeling, then what you have is art—or a novel called *War and Peace*.

Thus, connections that exist among the expository argument, history, and fiction show that the three modes work toward one purpose, and that all three are necessary because they encompass the totality of human experience that exists within the novel.

9

Genre and the Hero

The time has come to ask ourselves what kind of a book *War and Peace* is. Is it, after all, a regular novel, a "romance" (*roman*) set in a turbulent, indeed, epoch-making time in history? Is it an epic novel, a *roman-èpopoeia* (novel-epopee), so important in Russian critical terminology? Or is it an epoch unto itself, a unique, inimitable work of art that makes all its own rules as it goes along?

While none denies the uniqueness of the work, some readers have chosen sides. Among those who call the work a novel, R. F. Christian has stated his case most ably:

> It is impossible to define in the abstract what a novel *should* be like. . . . And there is no doubt that *War and Peace* has many of the characteristic features of earlier European novels. It has its love stories, happily crowned by marriage. It has many standard situations of entertainment and adventure. . . . It has to do with basic human emotions and conflicts—passion, jealousy, unrequited love, deep religious feeling, ambition, courage, thirst for adventure. It has its fair share of journeys, meetings and partings. . . . This is not to imply that *War and Peace* is like any novel in particular, but that it has enough recognizable thematic and other points

of contact to establish it as belonging to that loose and ample genre called the novel. (Christian, 113)

Christian's assertion opposes Tolstoy himself, who claimed, in several drafts of the introduction (*W&P*, 1362–74), that his work was not a novel, though it may resemble one in some ways. Tolstoy's main point was that he could not and would not set limits on the characters he had invented, limits like marriage or death, after which there would be no more interest in the narrative for the reader. Since one of the two male protagonists, Andrey, dies, and the other, Pierre, gets married, we need to ask why these endings do not impose the sort of limits on the text that would make it an ordinary novel. It may well be that Tolstoy did not mean that these were truly endings, but rather that they signified transitions to a different state, or dimension, and in that sense, a continuation. He had said that there are no real beginnings to any action; if so, then nothing ever really ends. As we know, the novel could have become an enormous prelude to the "real" story—that of the Decembrists of 1825 and their destinies.

From this perspective the work is finished in a way similar to that of the great classical epics, or at least *The Iliad*, and some readers have indeed elevated it to the status of an epic. Victor Terras sees the evolution of the work in terms similar to Boris Eikhenbaum's: "Conceived as a family novel with the thesis that familial, private concerns are at the bottom of what appear to be grand historical developments, it gradually became a historical epopoeia" (Terras, 355). He elaborates the epic traits of the work as follows:

> Like *The Iliad*, or the *Divine Comedy*, *War and Peace* produces a panoramic view of a whole country and of a historic era. . . . Its loving description of feasts, balls, hunting parties, and battles are epic. The unmotivated introduction of large numbers of characters who never return is epic, and so is the introduction of different levels of action, from the Olympian heights of royalty, to the war council of generals, and down to the battlefields where soldiers fight and die. Tolstoi's ample use of metonymic labels and other significant details may be also considered epic. . . . *War and Peace* is rich in Homeric similes. (Terras, 359)

L. D. Opul'skaya, one of the defenders of the term *roman-èpopoeia* much in favor among Russian scholars,[1] notes that the genre of *War and Peace* must be determined by norms other than the canonical West European classifications.[2] She claims that the most salient feature of the work is the "mutual interpenetration" of its novelistic and epic qualities. The work's genre freely and naturally combines detailed images of Russian country life, battle scenes, the author's narrative voice, and his philosophical thoughts (Opul'skaya, 144). By the same token, the genre embraces and incorporates the entirety of Russian life at the time and, essentially, for all time.

Arguments of this sort sound rather valedictory. Perhaps there is no particular need to attempt a classification of the work, especially if the effort does not bring us any closer to a better understanding and appreciation of the book.[3] Then again, the shape that this work cuts might be better outlined if it is compared with some more or less known genre category, a process that might be somewhat surprising.

Let us compare *War and Peace* with the traditional Greco-Roman epic in terms of structural equivalences. As already noted, Terras shows that Tolstoy debunked the classical epic canons pertaining to divine intervention, heroic leaders, and fate. Yet Tolstoy once said to Maksim Gorky that his *War and Peace*, "without false modesty, is like the *Iliad*."[4] The question is, on what terms might Tolstoy's novel be comparable to the classical genre of the epic?

In the classical epic, the actors are gods, heroes, and "the people." In strictly structural terms, the positions equivalent to those of the classical gods might be occupied by the two emperors, Napoleon and Alexander. They occupy a station in the social structure above all laws, and certainly there are passages, such as the parade review before the Battle of Austerlitz during which Nikolay is totally in awe of his tsar, in which a relationship of adoration, or unquestioning submission, seems to exist between these emperors and other humans. Yet, the crucial attributes of the gods—immortality and superior power, indeed, their "otherness" from humans—are denied in the novel, both in the narrative text, in which Napoleon is shown to be a despicable man mocked by his own ambitions, and Alexander, a mindless pawn of history, and in the expository essays, in which Tolstoy declares straight out that kings are nothing but history's slaves. In situations in which the emperors, like the gods of Greek epics, come to mingle with humans, they are either helpless, as when Alexander cries by the ditch at Austerlitz, or subject to Tolstoy's mordant satire. For instance, just before the Battle of Borodino Napolean washes his fat, white body and grunts with satisfaction like a piglet, while in contrast, the noble, plain Russian peasants put on clean white shirts in their readiness to die, not unlike the way the ancient Spartans combed their hair at Thermopylae. And whereas the Greek gods often participate in battles, giving very effective assistance to their favorite heroes, the two emperors could not possibly effect any sort of help. Obviously, unlike the gods, they are not adequate in their positions.

There is, however, another dimension in the relationship between humans and gods, at least in *The Iliad*. Without challenging the place of gods in his epic, Homer nevertheless manages to humanize them, giving them a reality that abstract figures of power could never have. According to George Steiner:

> In the *Iliad* divinity is quintessentially human. The gods are mortals magnified, and often magnified in a satiric vein. When wounded they howl louder than men, when they are enamoured their lusts are more consuming, when they flee before human spears their speed exceeds that of earthly chariots. But morally and intellectually the deities of the *Iliad* resemble giant brutes or malevolent children endowed with an excess of power. The actions of gods and goddesses in the Trojan War enhance the stature of man, for when odds are equal mortal heroes more than hold their own and when the scales are against them a Hector and an Achilles demonstrate that mortality has its own splendours. In lowering the gods to human values, the "first" Homer achieved not only an effect of comedy, though such an effect obviously contributes to the freshness and "fairy-tale" quality of the poem. Rather, he emphasized the excellence and dignity of heroic man.[5]

Tolstoy's Napoleon seems like an undersized brute and malevolent child. He does not possess any of the humanity that Homer gave to his gods, and it is this humanity that allows the gods to carry the weight of an epic in their confrontations with humans. In that sense, Tolstoy and Homer do come together—in both of their works the epic dimension resides precisely in the "excellence and dignity of heroic man"; the only difference is that Tolstoy's heroes are not from the socially superior class.

There is a power above the classical gods. These are the three Fates, Moiras, who weave the destinies of gods and men. As to what in *War and Peace* takes the place of these Moiras, or indeed, of destiny, one of the main plot devices in all literature, we must look again at to Tolstoy's ideas and the manner in which he embodies them in the fictional parts of the work. Tolstoy, we recall, said that history is made by all the people according to their own particular aims and via the demonstrations of such freedom of will as they may have. Thus, Tolstoy demythologizes the Moiras of Greece and makes them lose their status as either persons or symbols. Their power to control destiny becomes not an attribute of anyone, but a generalized presence in the fabric of life. Both in the fictional events and in the expository arguments, this generalized presence is transformed into particular actions and motivations. It also becomes cumulative, leading to the ultimate effects of many small causes, which, in their inevitability, take the place of destiny. If we say that Russia's destiny was its people, we are not merely being rhetorical—in *War and Peace* it is literally so.

Considered in this manner, the novel tends to acquire the character of an anti-epic, a parody. In addition, and perhaps more importantly, what we see in *War and Peace* is a general demythologizing of the mystery of being, a substitution of the myths that engender a holy awe of the universe with things that make common sense, yet without diminishing that awe. If we now look at specific features of the epic genre, we can see how this demythologization happens. The Greeks had their Mount Olympus, which served as the home of the gods, a mythological extension of the sky, a place of eternal serenity. In the novel the sky acquires a similar aspect, especially during moments of significant internal insight by the characters; yet, the sky stands for itself, and is not part of a larger myth. The most obvious example of the sky's importance, of course, is Andrey's new understanding as he lies wounded on the field of Austerlitz. A somewhat different sky, one that contains a discrete entity of destiny-shaping powers, is the sky with the comet that Pierre sees just after confessing his love to Natasha.

As we descend from Mount Olympus, we meet the heroes: Achilles, Ajax, Ulysses, Eneus, and a host of others. In the classical epic, these heroic characters are endowed with courage, skill, ambition, dedication, strength, and speed. Who occupies the place of these heroes in *War and Peace*? Tall and handsome officers and aristocrats, like Hector, do, but they are abysmally stupid where Ulysses was smart, cowardly where Achilles was brave, and vain where the Greek heroes had their virtue; in other words, just like the emperors, none of them is adequate to his position. It is amusing to read, for instance, how the main action device in the classical accounts of war—the personal duels between the heroes—is trivialized in the novel to produce the bumbling Pierre, who holds a gun he doesn't know how to shoot and wounds just such a mad "hero," Dolokhov, a fine parody of Achilles. There are more such trivialized duels. We can think of the Frenchman and the Russian artilleryman tugging at the two ends of a gun mop[6]; or of Rostov, in a parodic encounter with a Frenchman, throwing his pistol at him and running away; or of Pierre's entanglement with the French officer at the Battle of Borodino. In that skirmish they grabbed each other by the throat, and, "for some seconds they gazed with frightened eyes at one another's unfamiliar faces and both were perplexed at what they had done and what they were to do next" (*W&P*, 890). One does not recall any epic hero of old suffering from perplexity in the middle of combat.

Who, then, are the heroes of *War and Peace*? There really are no heroes; rather, there are men whose deeds emerge from the common fabric of life and who unconsciously enact the life-force that in Tolstoy is destiny. We have Captain Tushin, Timokhin, Kutuzov, Andrey (when he acts out of the simplicity of his heart), and, most important, a numberless host of plain line soldiers who, while always remaining simply human, accomplish deeds that would transcend and ennoble any ancient mythology. In the classical epic the people, of course, count for nothing. They are slaughtered en masse by the heroes, eaten by Polyphemus, and turned by Kirke into pigs. Certainly they have no such mobility of status as in *War and Peace*—a common man is always that, and no deeds of valor or wisdom can raise him to the position of a hero.

In accordance with their simplicity, the people who emerge to a moment's prominence in *War and Peace* lack the traditional heroic attributes of stature or beauty. Tushin, in fact, looks rather laughable with his bare feet and red nose; Karataev, whose name, Platon, is a fine ironic echo of the Greek philosopher, smells. One could almost say that if a character looks unprepossessing, or even downright ridiculous, chances are that he or she is of sterling virtue and quality. The Russian critic S. Bocharov has described the process by which those humble and ordinary folk become heroes of epic stature:

> The proportions have already been displaced, and a fantastic element, as if coming to this contemporary novel from the poetics of the heroic epic, from a *bylina*, permeates the realistic description. Measurements and scales change before our very eyes: the figure of the serf hunter is seen as if in two images at once. Small and modest to look at in terms of his everyday appearance, this figure nevertheless acquires a heroic size in our perception, completely outgrowing the limits of the room and expanding out into open space, to freedom. For this reason one becomes concerned about the walls which, it seems, will be knocked down, even though the giant in question stands humbly by one of the walls, close to the door, too short to reach the top of it. (Bocharov, 79)

The man Bocharev describes is Danilo, Rostov's head huntsman and kennelman. His position is very humble, but he is a master hunter and can dominate the proceedings by his awesome hunting skills and the sheer force of his personality. Danilo is in Rostov's room to consult about the hunt, and it is there that the "transformation" takes place. He represents the essence of the hidden strength of the Russian people and the heroic, epic dimensions to which they can suddenly grow when touched by the fearsome hand of war.

The main hero, Pierre, enters upon the stage in a most unprepossessing manner. He resembles a clown from commedia dell'arte: He is

nearsighted and fat, and wears narrow trousers and an enormous ruf-
fled collar, which supports his sweating head. He is not Pierre, but
Pierrot. The comic helplessness of Pierre is particularly noticeable
when contrasted to the elegance and intimidating pride of Andrey.[7] At
the same time, of course, the comparison with Andrey also brings out
Pierre's wisdom of the heart, as well as his deep inner energy, which
enables him to continue on his quest for truth. Pierre's "destiny" to
play Paris to "la belle Hélène," in light of the unequalled stupidity and
vulgarity of this substitute for the face that launched a thousand ships,
makes them both into wonderful parodies; indeed, this could be the
funniest idea of the whole novel. And yet his one true love, Natasha,
began to have the first stirrings of affection for him when she was still
but a little girl and observed that Pierre looked funny; upon that observation, she felt happy for no reason.[8] Moreover, Pierre is, after all, the
main hero, and together with Natasha he grows to dimensions that
encompass the largeness of the epoch.

The mock-heroic, anti-epic aspects of *War and Peace* change our
perspective on the work as an epopoeia, but this is not the whole
story. If we lay aside the classical epic, as well as Tolstoy's parodies of
it, we can still ask the question: What makes a truly epic story? The
drama, scale, and complexity of events and the epochal time in history
in which they take place are, of course, epic. The various particulars of
action, setting, and device mentioned by Victor Terras certainly contribute to the book's epic quality. The sense of the fullness of life in all
of its most minute details, and the awesome feeling that in *War and
Peace* we are confronted with both the macrocosm and microcosm of
being and that we then gradually discover that they are one is also
truly epic.

We might offer an additional criterion: An epic is a work in
which the personal destinies of its main heroes re-create in their own
measure the grand movements of the epochal time in which they live.
War and Peace is a work in which the main, or decisive mode of events
can be called a journey, or is governed by one, and in that it resembles
The Odyssey and *The Aeneid*, and also *The Iliad*. An oversimplification
could state that the action of the novel consists of Napoleon's thrust
into Russia—a journey of many miles—and his return. Tolstoy, of

course, gives Napoleon a failing grade as an earthly god, but the events that carry him in and out of Russia are truly epic in scale.

It is this journey, rather than the ordinary motivations of a novel—love, hate, ambition, and so on—that serves as the main catalyst to the life events of both Andrey and Pierre. Andrey is ultimately destroyed by Napoleon's invasion, but in the process he gains an ultimate understanding of death. Pierre escapes destruction, and is brought to his personal but at the same time universal understanding of life. For both, their destinies become a journey in the literal sense as well as the figurative, that is, a spiritual quest.

Such quest is a universal idea that has been articulated in life and fiction in various ways, from actual lives dedicated to a single purpose, as when hermits live in caves and seek a face-to-face encounter with God, to essential literary images, such as the search for the Holy Grail. As Victor Shklovsky observes, the unity of the novel does not emerge from the way it describes meetings and partings, loves and hates of a given set of people, but from the way it shows all the variety of life (Shklovsky, 423). In exposing this variety, Tolstoy has but a single purpose: To understand the relation of each personal destiny with the general history of humanity, which is itself but a single unyielding quest for something forever blessed and true that will bring us peace.

If we first consider Andrey, it does not appear that he is made by Tolstoy to be a seeker of unknown or hidden truths, either in the realm of feeling or intellect. When we first meet him, he seems bored by society and bent on military glory, or some other grand gesture. If motivated by vanity, such a yearning would seem not at all original— quite boring, in fact. Andrey, however, seems to be driven by some sort thirst for virtue, that supreme assertion of one's manhood before the eyes of fate that motivated the heroes of the Greek epics. Such a stance must ultimately be suicidal, because it is a confrontation between the absolute and mortality. Andrey, flag in hand, accomplishes his goal at Austerlitz, and yet he "dies" while looking at the absolute in the form of the sky, which tells him all is vanity, and yet also has a warmth, an understanding, as it were, of us poor ants down below. Death, while not as yet an awakening, begins to seem like a consolation.

Death is in attendance when Andrey's son is born, and parting is involved during the most poignant moments in his relationship with his father and sister. His love affair with Natasha, while deep, genuine, and highly poetic, is marked by separation, Natasha's frustration, and the pitiful episode of her infidelity. Their love fulfills itself only when Andrey lies dying. Curiously, that love then seems less personal and more symbolic. By that time the physically distant Natasha can no longer be his lover, and therefore she spiritually begins to resemble a mother, or at least the only mother figure Andrey has in the entire book.

Natasha's life also is affected by Napoleon's invasion, but instead of following the grand movements of the war, she undergoes a change in her place and function in the novel. At first she is just a happy sprite from provincial gentry, but as the epochal time and events grow around her, Tolstoy places her at certain junctures of events so that she can rise in our minds as a symbol of the inner strength of the country, and, by the end of the novel, embody Russia. The method of developing Natasha's stature is essentially the same one Tolstoy used to have the huntsman Danilo grow into a giant before our eyes. Let us note that none of the most marked events in Natasha's life have any inherently necessary connection with the war, yet they all change the outlines of Natasha's image. Andrey first meets her in springtime during a period of peace, and this meeting is not made necessary by the larger events to come. Against those events' dark, threatening background Natasha's image blends with the fresh vitality of springtime, and to Andrey she becomes the human, feminine configuration of a life-force that will not be denied. Along such a line of perception, the two contrasting views of the oak tree may also reach the level of a symbol and become, so to speak, a capsule history of Russia.

All these impressions—vitality, recovery, and, for Andrey, love— are encompassed in Natasha's image. Yet in Book 6 she is surrounded by negative markers: Andrey's disappointing dealings with Speransky and Arakcheev; Hélène's filthy social triumphs; Pierre's Masonic frustrations and despondency; the shabby "love story" between Berg and Vera; and later, old Bolkonsky's cruel insistence that the marriage be postponed, his torturing of Mary, and Andrey's departure. Nonetheless,

Natasha stands at the center of it all, luminous, white, enchanting, the magic core of all of Andrey's emotions. Again, it is not that Natasha in herself is particularly special, rather, she signifies something larger than herself. The hunting party, punctuated by Natasha's exuberant scream of victory and her graceful Russian dance, was created without any help from Napoleon's invasion. Nevertheless, it is there, at that hunting party, that we begin to feel in our bones the unconquerable strength of Russia, the exuberant force rising straight from the native soil. It is Natasha, the young goddess on the horse, the carefree dancer, who is "able to understand all that was in Anisya and in Anisya's father and mother and aunt, and in every Russian man and woman" (*W&P*, 564), who stands at the focal point of all this joyful power, and whose image extends to become an epic one. Her momentary seduction by Kuragin and subsequent nervous breakdown is the stuff of a flirtatious intrigue, not of a heroic epic. Yet, on the eve of 1812, her ordeal seems to prefigure, within the dimensions of a personal life, the rape and humiliation of Russia that will soon take place. It is in this context that her prayer for victory and forgiveness becomes, symbolically, an act of epic dimensions. Finally, her devotion to Andrey as he lies dying from his wounds could have been the same if he'd been ill in peacetime, but in the context of what she, as image, now represents, her actions can be viewed as the spirit of Russia blessing and parting from her dead. Natasha's eventual marriage to Pierre is not by any direct action a consequence of the war, yet in the hidden structure of the text it was preordained from the time when they looked "funny" to each other, and is the fulfillment of the book's implicit assertions. Natasha's dowdy ordinariness, prolific motherhood, clarity of purpose, simplicity, and devotion *is* the country, and it, this country, can rise to grand epic heights when the occasion calls for it. It would have rung false note for Tolstoy to have closed the book with anything more grandiose.

The general pattern of exposition and recovery that follows the outlines of the epic conflict flooding people's lives can also be seen in Pierre's development. Aside from his own internal complexities as an individual, there are external factors concerning Pierre's image as a literary hero that link him to the conventions of Russian romantic literature. The stereotypical leading man in romantic novels is rich, handsome, of superior intelligence, and also possessed of some inner flaw, or wound in the heart, which makes him mysterious and interesting. So Pechorin in Mikhail Lermontov's *Hero of Our Time* (1840) towers over all his adversaries. Tolstoy's Dolokhov has some of the same superman features, yet none of the intelligence nor manly charm of Pechorin. Nonetheless, he is still handsome, and still an army officer. The other examples of heroes, Berg and Drubetskoy, lose the content of their personalities, and keep only the handsome, tall exterior of the romantic hero. These two, having reached the pinnacle of manly beauty, possess no value at all, just like Kuragin and his sister Hélène. Andrey has much in him that recalls the older type of romantic hero,[9] as well as a deep, complex inner life and great nobility of character, but his deathward journey through the novel signifies the demise of the romantic character in Russian literature.

We might call these heroes the Apollonian types; although they are different from each other, at times unworthy, and often no more than parodies, they nevertheless constitute a set of modulations upon a governing idea that includes the notions of a controlling, comprehending mind; a decisive will to shape history; glamour; and romance. On the other side are the Dionysian characters: Kutuzov, Tushin, Timokhin, Denisov, the gnomic Karataev, the peasant Anisya, the "dragon" Akhrosimova, Count Rostov, and certainly Natasha and Pierre. The most characteristic notions encompassing this group include a spontaneous, instinctive perception of existence, an empathy with the organic continuum of life, and a certain knowledge beyond wisdom that penetrates more deeply to the source and meaning of all being than does the presumed superior mind of the traditional romantic hero.

The driving force in the development of Pierre's personality and his relationships with others can be understood in terms of two great tasks inherited from the literary conventions of the preceding romantic age—namely, experiencing a great love and engaging in a great quest. The two stories of love and marriage involving Pierre are both permeated with comic irony as well as melancholy, as if the tragic and comic masks of the Greek theater were exhibiting at the same time.

Pierre's marriage to Hélène's "creaking corset" is a truly sad piece of comic buffoonery, but it is important to see how, as their disastrous relationship develops, Pierre reveals attributes and feelings not natural to comic figures: intelligence, suffering, moral depth, nobility. His love for Natasha begins imperceptibly, as a slight nuance of feeling with a comic tinge, but we can feel its depth and truth in the couple's very comic helplessness, because they instinctively recognize their place in the enormity of the life-force surrounding them, and this feeling gives them epic dimensions within the structure of the book.

Don Quixote is Pierre's great comic predecessor in the literary tradition that represents life as a heroic quest. Pierre's great quest, however, is for nothing less than the entire meaning of life. His journey toward truth begins with alcohol, women, hazy idealistic notions about Napoleon, and so on. As he reaches his bleak crossroads, with barren thoughts spinning uselessly in his head, we can see that the turning point in his life is now approaching. Yet, it is also surrounded with markers, such as Pierre's first meeting with Bazdeev, that demythologize the spiritual quest and lower it to the level of the comic. Pierre's subsequent entrance to the Masonic order is accompanied by similar degrading markers in which Tolstoy uses his famous method of "making strange" to deprive the supposedly profound and sacred ceremony of all meaning (as he also deprived the opera performance that Natasha saw of the attributes of "high art").

Pierre's great quest unfolds as it moves through his absurd notion that he is fated to kill Napoleon, then takes him to the battlefield of Borodino, and finally sets him wandering in Moscow's burning streets. Between his meeting with Bazdeev and his experiences at Borodino, he seems to have completed the circle from nothing to nothing. Yet Pierre does learn something of great importance—namely, that his great yearning for a "world of eternal, solemn and calm thoughts," (W&P, 1001) like Andrey's sky and like the Masonic philosophy, is capable of being fulfilled in the world of the simple Russian people he saw dying with calm fortitude at Borodino. What the peasants always knew and what Pierre strove to learn from the Masons comes together in his experience, and he is ready to meet Karataev, and the great watery globe, his own Holy Grail.

The comic Pierre is essentially different from the standard buffoon in that his human imperfections both engender and reveal his great and gentle humanity. The heroic Pierre is also different from the stereotypical romantic knight. The trials and tribulations of the traditional heroes are grounded in and somewhat limited by a literary device, for despite all the hero's hardships, his image, an entity set by convention, remains sacrosanct. Pierre, on the other hand, recognizes in his consciousness a new dimension of human existence that has not been defined by any existing literary tradition and therefore has the full impact of significant reality.[10] As Pierre accomplishes his transition, we come to understand that his life has parallelled the tremendous epic accomplishment of a new kind of nation-hero. It is not a nation that follows great leaders to victory, but one that rose from its knees, having touched the native ground in its hour of darkness, to become a legend, all the while sustaining its human simplicity.

Gary Saul Morson shifts attention away from genre classifications to a different mode of reading. Morson notes that *War and Peace* has no real beginning, middle, or end; that the motivation of action by causality is really irrelevant to the telling of the plot, and so important events seem insignificant and vice versa, and that in general the work makes a parody out of historical fiction or any other genre. The thrust of Morson's argument is that the process of building the novel repeats the processes Tolstoy sees as shaping history. Morson calls these processes "creation by potential," as opposed to developments made in accordance with some abstractly conceived and superimposed laws. A full accounting of all causes of events is beyond calculation, and anything that fails to take place is as real and important as what does happen. Tolstoy's text seizes the moment, perceives a configuration of opportunity, and makes choices unhampered by some logical model. The book presents a process of realization of some potentials from an infinite number. The spontaneous actions of cavalrymen like Nikolay Rostov; the momentary decisions of field commanders; mass action by the people, often against all logic—all these can be cited to support Morson's argument. What we have in the novel are plausible sequences of events without any explanation as to why they occurred and equally plausible others did not. Morson calls this principle a "polyphony of incident" (Morson, 186). Seeing time and cause as a random aggregate of realities, Morson also feels that in Tolstoy's works a character is "not a system but an aggregate." A character "is a cluster of habits and memories, which incorporate and 'excorporate' elements of the random in an endless succession describable by no overarching design" (Morson, 205). Such an uncertain and diffuse flow of consciousness and habit makes it practically impossible to develop a moral code that could be applied like a grid upon the whole of life in order to determine one's right conduct at each moment. Instead we have an inner "judge" in Karataev and, in the end, in Pierre Bezukhov, a judge that instantly, unerringly determines the right course of action at any moment, just as an animal, as Tolstoy once said, when thirsty, unerringly finds water to drink. It is not that Pierre has become infallible—such a concept operates only if either right or wrong choices are possible. What happens to Pierre is that he becomes attuned, unconsciously, to the way things are; conscious decisions are moot. Thus, we neither have nor lack free will; what is happening is happening, and we contribute to it by what we do or don't do. The state of mind that can permit such knowledge corresponds to the divine light inside us; this is what it means to "have God in your heart," as a simple peasant tells Konstantin Levin toward the end of the latter's fruitless search for meaning in *Anna Karenina*. Richard F. Gustafson has elegantly connected this point to the nature of Tolstoy's creative imagination: "He [Tolstoy] receives a flashlight pencil as a gift and pronounces it an 'emblem of life' because it works like life: 'unscrew it, set free what covers the light in your soul and you will live in a light that illuminates for you what you need to see and to know in order to act and only what you need in order to act.'. . . The humble object embodies and reveals the moral and spiritual truth of all being in God. The imagination that saw this flashlight pencil as an 'emblem of life' created *War and Peace* and *Anna Karenina*."[11]

Any traditional genre description is in essence a set of require-ments that the text must meet. Any deviation invites new subclassifica-tions, and research on Tolstoy abounds with these. Moreover, any action by the protagonists does eventually come down to a choice between right and wrong, or to a point in which destructive forces inside a character make him or her either incapable of recognizing the right thing, or incapable of choosing it. Without some such framework, it is difficult to avoid bringing a "baggy monster" of a novel into the world; if life is a flow of random information, then there should be ways of processing that information in some direction. There should be a computer chip, an algorithm, inside us that shapes information not according to the inherent randomness of reality, but according to the pattern in the chip itself.

Notes and References

1. Tolstoy's Russia: Between East and West

1. Indeed, some scholars feel that without these concrete biographical sources the novel might not have been written. See, for instance, Boris Eikhenbaum, *Lev Tolstoy: Kniga pervaya* (Leo Tolstoy: Volume one) (Leningrad-Moscow: Priboy [The Surf] Publishing House, 1928); hereafter cited in text as Eikhenbaum I.

2. This group of eighteenth-century French intellectuals, including Jean Jacques Rousseau, Charles de Montesquieu, François Voltaire, and Denis Diderot, was called *Les Encyclopédistes* because of their collaboration on a monumental work called *Encyclopédie; ou dictionnaire raisoné des sciences, des arts et des métiers*, which Diderot brought to conclusion in 1772. The encyclopedia promoted a spirit of skepticism, scientific determinism, and rationalism. It attacked abuses of power by the ruling classes, among them, aristocracy and the clergy. Tremendously influential, this work did a great deal to prepare the ground for the French Revolution.

3. Victor Terras et al., eds., *Handbook of Russian Literature* (New Haven: Yale University Press, 1985), 517.

4. The Decembrists, composed of idealistic Russian army officers, noblemen, and intellectuals, staged a coup in St. Petersburg on 14 December 1825 in an attempt to establish a constitutional monarchy; the coup failed and they were quickly crushed, tried, exiled to Siberia for long terms, or executed. At no time did their forces comprise more than a small minority of the Russian military and civilian middle classes.

5. Turgenev quite succinctly described Tolstoy's anti-Westernism: "He [Tolstoy] finds the French rhetoric repulsive, but even more he hates rationality, system, science, in a word, Germans. His entire last novel [*War and Peace*] is built on this enmity to the mind, to knowledge and to awareness of self." Quoted in Eikhenbaum I, 381.

6. For Dostoyevski, the salvation of all humanity as a spiritual idea became closely intertwined with the military and political growth of Russia as a historical fact. In one of his articles on art (F.M. Dostoevskij, "Rjad statej o russkoj literature," *F.M. Dostoevskij ob iskusstve* [F. M. Dostoyevski, "A Set of Articles on Russian Literature" in "F. M. Dostoyevski on Art"] [Moscow: Iskusstvo, 1973], 349), Dostoyevski says that Ivan III, waiting in a little hut for his decisive battle against the Tartars to begin, had the foresight to perceive that this battle would not only be a matter of dominating the East, but that it would also be the dawn of the new world order in which Russia would save and enlighten the world. Dostoyevski calls this thought an "original" real idea of the kind that distinguishes great nations from insignificant ones.

7. S. Bocharov, *Roman L. Tolstogo "Voina i mir"* (Leo Tolstoy's novel "War and Peace") (Moscow: State Belles Lettres Publishing House, 1963), 23–24; hereafter cited in text as *Bocharov.*

2. *War and Peace:* The Towering Novel

1. See A. Saburov, *"Voina i Mir" L. N. Tolstogo: Problematika i poetika* (L. N. Tolstoy's *War and Peace*: Issues and poetics) (Moscow: Moscow State University, 1959), 332–33.

2. See Boris Eikhenbaum, *Lev Tolstoy: Kniga vtoraya* (Lev Tolstoy: Volume 2) (Leningrad: Priboy [The Surf] Publishing House, 1931), 318; hereafter cited as Eikhenbaum II.

3. Aylmer Maude, *The Life of Tolstoy* (1908; reprint, New York: Oxford University Press, 1987), vol. 1, *The First Fifty Years*, 432; hereafter cited in text as Maude.

4. In 1865 Tolstoy wrote to fellow writer Boborykin: "If I were told that I could write a novel in which I should set forth the apparently correct attitudes toward all social questions, I would not devote even two hours of work to such a novel, but if I were told that what I shall write will be read in twenty years by the children of today and they will weep and smile over it and will fall in love with life, I would devote all my life and all my strength to it." See Lev Tolstoy, *War and Peace*, ed. George Gibian, trans. Aylmer Maude (New York: Norton, 1966), 1360; hereafter cited as *W&P.*

5. Leo Tolstoy, *Polnoe sobranie sochinenij* (Complete collection of works), V. G. Chertkov et al., editors, (Moscow: State Publishing House, 1928–58) vol. 46, 69; hereafter cited as *PSS.*

6. In his essay "Tolstoy, Seer of the Flesh," Dmitry Merezhkovsky analyzes Tolstoy via the distinctions made by apostle Paul—those of the physical, spiritual, and natural man: "Tolstoy is the greatest depictor of this physico-spiritual region in the natural man; that side of the flesh which approaches the spirit, and that side of the spirit which approaches the flesh, the mysterious border region where the struggle between the animal and the God in man takes place.

Therein lies the struggle and the tragedy of his own life. He is a 'man of the sense,' half-heathen, half-Christian; neither to the full." In *Tolstoy: A Collection of Critical Essays*, ed. Ralph E. Matlaw (Englewood Cliffs, N.J.: Prentice Hall, 1967), 64.

3. Kicking the Mountain: The Critics' Response

1. Tolstoy's letter to P. D. Boborykin, July or August, 1865. See *W&P*, 1359. However, as noted by Ralph Matlaw in "Mechanical Structure and Inner Form: A Note on *War and Peace* and *Dr. Zhivago*," the second epilogue, as a philosophical essay, does suggest that Tolstoy wished to impose some ideological generalization upon the work. See *Symposium* (Winter 1962): 288–95.

2. Socially oriented readers also completely failed to grasp Tolstoy's point. According to Boris Eikhenbaum, "The general opinion was that Tolstoy had scattered himself among petty trifles and details not bound together by any general idea." See Eikhenbaum II, 117.

3. *W&P*, 1366; from Lev Tolstoy, "Some Words about *War and Peace*," first published in 1868.

4. The impression of incoherence also may be due in part to the fact that the novel first came out in separate installments in the years 1865–66 in the journal the *Russian Messenger*. The entire text, still under the title *1805*, was not published until 1866. For an illuminating commentary, see Gary Saul Morson, *Hidden in Plain View: Narrative and Creative Potentials in "War and Peace"* (Stanford, Calif.: Stanford University Press, 1987), 57–58; hereafter cited in the text as Morson.

5. Dated March 16/28,1864. Borisov was a friend of the poet Afanasy Fet and of Tolstoy. Quoted in: Eikhenbaum II, 266.

6. To be fair, in 1880, writing to M. About, editor of *Le XIXe Siècle*, Turgenev praised Tolstoy emphatically: "The spirit of an epic fills this vast work; in it the public and private life of Russia during the first years of our century is rendered by the hand of a true master. . . . It may be that the profound originality of Count Tolstoy by its sheer strength will impede a sympathetic and swift understanding [as it happened with Turgenev himself!—R.S.] of his novel by foreign readers; but I repeat—and I would be happy if my words were taken with confidence—this is a great work by a great writer—and this is real Russia." See *W&P*, 1388–89.

7. Eikhenbaum II, 266.

8. Quoted in Eikhenbaum II, 393. Tolstoy himself was quite aware that other Russian writers also shared in this "unique Russian genre." In "Some Words about *War and Peace*" he said: "The history of Russian literature since the time of Pushkin not merely affords many examples of such deviation from European forms, but does not offer a single example of the contrary. From

Gogol's *Dead Souls* to Dostoyevski's *House of the Dead*, in the recent period of Russian literature there is not a single artistic prose work rising at all above mediocrity, which quite fits into the form of a novel, epic or story" (*W&P*, 1366).

9. "*Anna Karenina* kak fakt osobogo znachenija" (*Anna Karenina* as a Fact of Special Significance) in S. P. Bychtov, ed., *Dostoevsky ob iskusstve* (Dostoyevski on Art), (Moscow: "Art" [iskusstvo] Publishing House, 1973) 279.

10. N. G. Chernyshevsky, "Tolstoy's *Childhood and Adolescence* and His War Stories," as quoted in *L. N. Tolstoy v russkoi kritike* (L. N. Tolstoy in Russian criticism) (Moscow: State Belles Lettres Publishing House, 1952), 93.

11. According to Boris Sorokin, "Mikhailovsky implied a periodic failure of the connection between the two sides of Tolstoy's brain. As a result, Tolstoy was literally functioning as a man whose right hand did not know what his left hand was doing." See Sorokin, *Tolstoy in Prerevolutionary Russian Criticism* (Columbus: Ohio State University Press, 1979), 172–73; hereafter cited as Sorokin.

12. Among recent readers, Boris Sorokin also thinks that in his art Tolstoy "unintentionally reflected the amoral, intuitive 'pagan' mentality of many Russians" (Sorokin, 20). Victor Terras, in *A History of Russian Literature*, also speaks of Tolstoy's "amoral vitalism." (New Haven: Yale University Press, 1985.) Tolstoy, intensely concerned with moral issues all his life, might also eventually have perceived a lack of fundamental moral fiber in his own works, and he may have denounced them mainly for this reason in his essay "What Is Art?" (1897).

13. Dmitry Merezhkovsky, *Dostoevsky and Tolstoy* (New York: G. P. Putnam, 1912), 213.

14. John Bayley, *Tolstoy and the Novel* (New York: Viking Press, 1966), 72; hereafter cited as Bayley.

15. This quotation is in Lenin's most influential article, "Tolstoy as the Mirror of the Russian Revolution" (1905), in which he exposes Tolstoy's inner contradictions with scathing rhetoric. In V. I. Lenin, *Tolstoy and His Time* (New York: International Publishers, 1952) 3–9.

16. For a concise and still-standard discussion of Russian formalism, see Victor Erlich, *Russian Formalism: History-Doctrine* (The Hague: Mouton, 1969).

17. See Viktor Shklovsky, *Material i stil' v romane L'va Tolstogo "Voina i Mir"* (Substance and style in Leo Tolstoy's novel *War and Peace*) (Moscow: The "Federation" Publishing House, 1928), Shklovsky's main study of Tolstoy; hereafter cited as Shklovsky 1928.

18. See Viktor Shklovsky, *Lev Tolstoy* (Moscow: Young Guard, 1963); hereafter cited as Shklovsky 1963.

19. Perhaps one should say "pre-functional identity"—the identity things had as themselves, before any function or sets of functions were attached to them and even overwhelmed them.

20. As it pertains to *War and Peace*, Shklovsky explains the term "making strange" as follows: "Tolstoy was able to create a literary system which differed greatly from the usual system, from the customary transmission of reality and which could be interpreted as historical because of this very thing. But for this system he no longer needed historical facts. The discovery of this new method consisted in the device of 'making strange,' that is taking a thing out of normal perception; in order thus to remove a thing from normal perception, we can change its appearance and we can change the method of its rendering" (*W&P*, 1434–35).

21. For a fuller discussion of this episode in *War and Peace*, see R. Silbajoris, *Tolstoy's Aesthetics and His Art* (Columbus, Ohio: Slavica, 1991), 141–42; hereafter cited as Silbajoris.

22. See in particular Eikhenbaum II. In response, R. F. Christian disputes this analysis on the grounds that all the elements of *War and Peace* were there from the very beginning: "All these ingredients are alluded to in one form or another in the earliest plans and drafts of the novel and make nonsense of the suggestion that they—or some of them—were necessitated by a later elevation of genre." See his *Tolstoy's "War and Peace": A Study* (Oxford: Clarendon Press, 1962), 121; hereafter cited as Christian.

23. Eikhenbaum gives the following summary of the main influences: "Proudhon [Pierre Joseph, 1809–65] and de Maistre [Joseph, 1763–1852] were useful to Tolstoy for the philosophy of war and for the treatment of Napoleon; Pogodin [Mikhail Petrovich, 1800–75] helped him with concepts of history and the philosophy of history; together with Pogodin, and as a helper in the development of philosophical-historical ideas, there was the mathematician and conservative philosopher Urusov [Sergei S., 1827–97]." See Eikhenbaum II, 347.

24. Victor Terras, though not a Soviet critic, improves upon the Soviet term and gives it more grandeur by calling *War and Peace* "a historical epopoeia." See Victor Terras, *The Age of the Novel* (Yale University Press, 1991), 355.

25. E. N. Kupreyanova, "O problematike i zhanrovoy prirode romana L. Tolstogo 'Voina i mir'" (On the issues and genre definition of Tolstoy's Novel "War and Peace"), *Russkaya literatura* (Russian literature) 1 (1985), 161–72.

26. Henry James, preface to *The Tragic Muse* (1908), as quoted in *W&P*, 1396.

27. As quoted in Gary Saul Morson, *Hidden in Plain View: Narrative and Creative Potentials in "War and Peace"* (Stanford, Calif.: Stanford University Press, 1987) 78; hereafter cited as Morson.

28. Edward Wasiolek, *Tolstoy's Major Fiction* (Chicago, Ill.: University of Chicago Press, 1978), 102; hereafter cited as Wasiolek.

29. S. C. Bocharov puts it in another way. The Napoleonic War replaced the "falsely important" (presumably philosophical) themes, and brought forth the simple and true values—youth, health, love, enjoyment of art, the closeness of the people, and the joy of communication. That, says Bocharov, is the idea of the novel: "*War and Peace* is dedicated to these *certain* things in human life—these are the things that serve as the topic and the aim of artistic embodiment" (Bocharov, 17).

30. Philip Rahv, "Tolstoy: The Green Twig and the Black Trunk," in his *Image and Idea: Fourteen Essays on Literary Themes* (New York: New Directions, 1949), 71.

4. Conception and Growth of the Novel

1. This episode is described in "Yasnaya Polyana in November and December," *PSS*, vol. 8, 101–2, and is cited in detail by Boris Eikhenbaum in Eikhenbaum II, 231–36. Eikhenbaum notes that even at that time Tolstoy had "anti-historical" sentiments, believing that meaningful events exist only on the plane of personal experience. Perhaps even more interesting is the fact that the roots of Tolstoy's many thoughts about art and the topics for some of his stories, such as "Hadzhi Murat" (1904), also go back to this Yasnaya Polyana period, a time when Tolstoy thought he had given up literature. See also Silbajoris, chapter 2.

2. See Tolstoy, *Childhood, Boyhood, Youth* (New York: Penguin, 1964), 34. These ants, running about purposefully in a miniature world, may well represent the first source of the image of the antlike movements of soldiers at Austerlitz, perceived as so meaningless to the wounded Andrey; it may also be an inspiration for the extended Moscow-beehive metaphor that Tolstoy employs to describe the city as Napoleon was about to enter it.

3. Richard Freeborn comments on the formation of the novel: "In *War and Peace* Tolstoy multiplies what is in essentials the formal scheme of *Childhood* by employing the same principle of immediacy of factual description couched or framed in short scenes. We are not concerned with the causes or consequences of the scene; we are concerned with the immediacy, the pure present time, of the fictive experience." See his *The Rise of the Russian Novel: Studies in the Russian Novel from "Eugene Onegin" to "War and Peace"* (Cambridge: Cambridge University Press, 1973), 210.

4. In one of his prefaces to *War and Peace*, Tolstoy faces a chilling thought: "Why did millions of people kill one another when it has been known since the world began that it is physically and morally bad to do so? Because it was such an inevitable necessity that in doing it men fulfilled the elemental zoological law which bees fulfill when they kill one another in autumn,

and which causes male animals to destroy one another. One can give no other reply to that terrible question" (*W&P*, 1372). This statement stands alone, without elaboration either in the novel or in other comments by Tolstoy. It is almost as if Tolstoy had lifted one corner of the curtain and seen truth as a nightmare, and dropped the curtain immediately.

5. Some critics, particularly Bakhtin, thought that in this way Tolstoy is radically different from Dostoyevski, whose heroes have no past. But one might also remember that Anna Karenina is first presented to us without a past, in a momentary temporal frame, as she steps down from the train and meets Vronsky's eyes, and they fall head over heels in love.

6. In Tolstoy's own explanation, this retreat in time sounds a little puzzling. He said: "I was ashamed to write about our triumph . . . without having described our failures and our shame. . . . If the cause of our victory was not accidental, but lay in the essence of the character of the Russian people and army, then that character must be expressed still more clearly in the period of failures and defeats" (*W&P*, 1364). The problem is that the Russian people and army in 1805, as depicted by Tolstoy, do not in any way show the qualities that could explain their victory in 1812, except perhaps in the single episode in which Russian soldiers march before the Battle of Austerlitz, and in which their spontaneous, joyful singing carries with it an impression of a joyful strength and readiness (*W&P*, 126).

7. Prince S. S. Urusov (1827–97), a soldier, chess player, mathematician, historical philosopher, and all-around maverick who devoted much thought to the 1812 period, first met Tolstoy in Sevastopol', where together they defended the Russian bastions against the British. Urusov's conservative views of history resembled in some aspects those of Tolstoy.

8. See *U Tolstogo: Yasnopolyanskie zapiski D. P. Makovickogo* (At Tolstoy's: The Yasnaya Polyana notes of D.P. Makovicky), vol. 1 (Moscow: Science, 1979), 200. The idea of the goodness of death and one's serene surrender to it was already present in Tolstoy's early story "Three Deaths" (1858), in which, faced with death, a neurotic aristocrat prays in vain and suffers agonies of fear, a peasant calmly passes into it, and a tree falls magnificently, in what seems like a proud assent to the life-and-death cycle of nature.

5. The World of Perceptions
1. Charanne Carroll Clarke, "Aspects of Impressionism in Chekhov's Prose," in *Chekhov's Art of Writing: A Collection of Critical Essays*, ed. Paul Debreczeny and Thomas Eekman (Columbus, Ohio: Slavica, 1977), 123.

2. There are certain affinities between Chekhov and Tolstoy as writers. Chekhov, for instance, shared Tolstoy's lack of interest in intellectualizing life and reluctance to structure it to fit preconceived ideas. He also acquired from Tolstoy some storytelling techniques, notably that of depicting the world from

inside a character's mind rather than describing it from the narrator's point of view.

3. This process of creation through reflection actually characterizes Tolstoy's own creative method. He articulated it very early in his career, in an 1851 diary entry.

4. A huge example of such fakery, in Tolstoy's eyes, was the entire tradition of Western art, which he called "counterfeit"; Tolstoy felt it had no ability to convey to another person, or "infect" him or her with the actual feeling experienced by the artist.

5. See Baudelaire, "Correspondances":

> La Nature est un temple où de vivants piliers
> Laissent parfois sortir de confuses paroles;
> L'homme y passe à travers des forêts des symboles
> Qui l'observent avec des regards familiers.

> Nature is a temple where from the living pillars
> Confused utterances part at times;
> One passes there across forests of symbols
> Which observe you with a familiar look.

Charles Baudelaire, *Les Fleurs du Mal* (The Flowers of Evil) (Lausanne: Librairie Payot, 1946), 18. Translation mine.

6. For an elaboration on the complexity of Nikolay's feelings, see Silbajoris, 60–61.

7. We may note that earlier, during Andrey's first visit to Otradnoe, the Rostovs' estate, at night in his room he heard Natasha say through the window that she felt like "putting my arms around my knees, straining tight, as tight as possible, and flying away" (*W&P*, 461). The same semantic marker, flying through the air, signals both the beginning of Andrey's love for Natasha, and now at the opera, her surrender to Kuragin's temptation.

8. The metaphor of a hunted wolf extends beyond Tolstoy's text to other references in literature. There is, for instance, a well-known fable by Ivan Andreevich Krylov (1769–1844) about a wolf captured in the sheep-sty; it is made quite clear that the wolf is Napoleon.

9. A meal of rice and raisins, the *Kutya*, is traditionally eaten at funeral repasts in Russia.

10. It is interesting to compare Petya's falling to his death with Natasha's flying through the air as the first stirrings of sexual life awaken in her. Another possible link is Natasha's wondrous dancing to her "uncle's" music after the hunt in Book 7. Petya sleeps through it all and is brought home still sleeping "like a log." Thus music and the deathlike state of deep sleep, and music and death, and also brother and sister are brought together in a structural configuration.

11. *W&P*, 1174. Petya's death may also be prefigured in Tolstoy's early Caucasus story "The Raid" (1852), in which a young and foolish officer, Alanin, anxious to show off his courage, dashes into the forest with his saber in the air, only to be killed. See also Laura Jepsen, *From Achilles to Christ: The Myth of the Hero in Tolstoy's "War and Peace"* (Tallahassee: Jepsen, 1978) 126–27.

12. According to Victor Shklovsky, an early image of the globe exists in *The Yasnaya Polyana Notes* (1862), in one variant of the article "Who Is to Learn from Whom: The Peasant Children from Us, or We from Peasant Children?" Tolstoy thought of a "perfect, mathematically true, living globe, developing under its own energy. . . . This globe is the image of perfection, but it must grow just up to the limit of size set for it, among innumerable similar freely growing globes" (Shklovsky, 405–6). For Tolstoy, these "globes" meant the children—the subjects of his educational efforts. It is easy to see in them the embryonic vision of the water droplets in Pierre's dream.

13. *U Tolstogo. Yasnopolyanskie zapiski D. P. Makovickogo, 1904–1910* (At Tolstoy's. The Yasnaya Polyana notes of D. P. Makovicky, 1904–1910), Literaturnoe nasledstvo No. 69, J. P. Berdnikov et al., editors (Moscow: Science, 1979).

6. Perspectives: Author, Reader, Character

1. This chapter takes place in 1812 at the war front; Hendrikhovna is the German wife of an army doctor with the troops. The focal point is a scene in which she is dispensing tea to cheerful Russian hussars who surround her like some faithful subjects in adoration of their queen. Her simplicity and plump, benevolent motherliness evoke a distant echo of Platon Karataev, the Russian peasant soldier whom Pierre Bezukhov met in French captivity, while in terms of group dynamics she looks like an ironic mirror image of Madame Sherer amidst her guests in chapter 1. The cheerful corpulent Anisya of chapter 6, who dispenses tasty Russian country fare to the hunters, is another link.

2. It is important to remember, however, as R. F. Christian points out (Christian, 44) that Karataev's proverbs, though seeming to emerge from him spontaneously, were carefully culled by Tolstoy from the folklorist and lexicographer Vladimir Dal's *Proverbs of the Russian People* (St. Petersburg, Moscow, 1800–1882).

3. We may observe the consistency of Tolstoy's image: In the argument, the totality of things determining our actions is round like the globe. Karataev, the temporary individual configuration of this totality, is himself round like a globe, and Pierre's dream, one that helps him understand that all existence is God, represents this insight in the form of a silvery globe. Further, the Battle of Borodino begins with round puffs of smoke from artillery shells, one of which will mean Andrey's death.

4. Amusingly, Tolstoy used the device of the "meaningfully meaningless" glance earlier, in Book 1, in describing Pierre's dying father: "When Pierre came up the count was gazing straight at him, but with a look the significance of which could not be understood by mortal man. Either this look meant nothing but that as long as one has eyes they must look somewhere, or it meant too much" (*W&P*, 86). One might consider this an effective device in conveying the state of mind of a person facing impending events so enormous that they are beyond comprehension—the coming of a fateful battle, or the coming of death.

5. Tolstoy originally intended to have Andrey killed soon after this scene, at Austerlitz. The departure scene remained the same in later versions and therefore carries the shadow of Andrey's death into his later life. Nonetheless, this actually is the last time Andrey sees his father.

6. This chain continues as a submerged thread in the novel's texture to the moment at Borodino in which Andrey is mortally wounded by an exploding cannon shell. Remembering his emotional emptiness at Schöngraben, we are particularly touched by the sudden rush of love for life that Andrey feels as he is looking at the spinning ball (*W&P*, 904).

7. *W&P*, 208. In *Paradise Lost*, John Milton speaks of Hell as a burning place where "from those flames/ No light, but rather darkness visible/ Served only to discover sights of woe." John Milton, *Paradise Lost and Paradise Regained.* James H. Hanford, ed. (New York: Franklin Watts, Inc., n.d.), 7. Tolstoy completes the image by creating his audible darkness.

8. *W&P*, 378. At this point Aylmer Maude makes an important observation in a footnote: "Here, in the year 1864, we have the questions which fourteen years later produced a crisis in Tolstoy's own life and caused him to write *A Confession.*"

9. In a Tolstoyan text even this quite ordinary information seems to acquire a symbolic dimension as we realize that Pierre will indeed "change horses" at this point in his life, after meeting Bazdeev.

10. See *W&P*, 738: "Then it occurred to him [Pierre]: if the answer to the question were contained in his name, his nationality would also be given in the answer. So he wrote *Le russe Besuhof* and adding up the numbers got 671. This was only five too much, and five was represented by *e*, the very letter edited from the article *Le* before the word *Empereur*. By omitting the *e*, though incorrectly, Pierre got the answer he sought. *L'russe Besuhof* made 666." Later Pierre decides that this was the indication that he would kill Napoleon and end the reign of the Beast. According to such Masonic calculations, we could conclude that Pierre failed to kill Napoleon because of a grammatical error in his name, and that could amount to a truly Tolstoyan satirical comment on the nature of causality in history.

11. We should note, however, that neither Pierre nor Tolstoy considers the Masonic teachings to be completely worthless. Pierre's eventual peace of mind has strong elements of the Masonic worldview in it.

12. We must note, however, one poignant and radical difference between Andrey and Dolokhov: Andrey has no mother. Of course, Dolokhov's dear mother is never mentioned again; having served her function, she is discarded. In this way she reminds us ironically of Napoleon's "ma pauvre mère," to whom he dedicated his presumed victory in Moscow. See *W&P*, 973.

13. *W&P*, 341. The dear mother of a hard-eyed villain or hero is, of course, a romantic and sentimental cliché, and the invalid daughter, sister, or wife is also a beloved (or tortured, or both) icon in the works of Dostoyevski. The lame Lizaveta is whipped twice a week by Captain Lebyadkin of *The Possessed*, and, in *Crime and Punishment*, Raskolnikov had thought of marrying the hunchbacked daughter of his landlady. Such harsh visions seem much more at home in Dostoyevski's world than in Tolstoy's.

14. The nurse who sang Andrey to sleep is a literary relative of the Russian poet Mikhail Lermontov's mother, who also sang lullabies to him, and whom Lermontov lost when he was two. In one of Lermontov's poems this mother becomes an angel, singing and carrying a soul from heaven to be born on earth. Lermontov, Andrey, and Tolstoy himself (whose parents died when he was a young boy) are thus three related orphans in a combined literary and actual world. The memory of childhood as the best time in life also comes to the dying hero in Tolstoy's later story *The Death of Ivan Ilyich*.

7. Recurrences and Linkages

1. A similar term, *situation rhyme*, has been employed previously by J. M. Meijer in *Situation Rhyme in a Novel of Dostoyevsky* ('SGravenhage: Mouton, 1958). R. F. Christian discusses it in *Tolstoy's "War and Peace"*, 131ff.

2. Looking ahead in Tolstoy's works, we see that Ivan Ilyich dies in his study on the same sort of sofa. Tolstoy had just this kind of a large leather sofa in his study in Yasnaya Polyana, and many a time the writer, feeling unwell, had lain on it.

3. We could note, as a counterpoint to Natasha's firm step, Pierre's sinking feeling as he tries to bring to action the Masonic principles he has been studying: "Amid the turmoil of his activities and distractions, however, Pierre at the end of a year began to feel that the more firmly he tried to rest upon it, the more the Masonic ground on which he stood gave way under him" (*W&P*, 474). It is amusing to remember just how big, round, and heavy Pierre was. Pierre's feet also come to the fore in his barefoot march through snow and mud during his captivity.

4. *W&P*, 387. Very often in Tolstoy's works it is the superfluous detail that makes the reading interesting. "Skull and lamp" without the teeth and cavities would be too abstract, too much like the materialization of a pure idea, to permit any suggestion of its absurdity, which becomes possible only

when things become concrete and descend to a level at which abstract ideas do not dwell. This detail is another example of "making strange": The sudden interest in the teeth and cavities of a symbolic skull makes us feel as though we are looking at the conventions of life without sharing their assumed meaning, thus making these same conventions pointless and incapable of signifying. And that, of course, is Tolstoy's message about the masonic order and its mysteries.

5. The structure of this paradoxical statement is repeated at least once more in Tolstoy, namely, in *The Death of Ivan Ilyich*, at the beginning of the biographical survey of Ilyich's life: "The story of Ivan Ilyich's life was of the simplest, most ordinary and therefore most terrible" (Tolstoy, *The Cossacks/ Happy Ever After/ The Death of Ivan Ilyich* [New York: Penguin, 1960], 109). The context is similar, for Andrey, like Ilyich, is standing at death's door, although he may not know it yet, and is engaging in a stocktaking of his life.

6. V. Ermilov, *Tolstoy romanist* (Tolstoy the novelist) (Moscow:State Belles Lettres Publishing House, 1965), 124–25.

7. *Lay of the Host of Igor'*, in describing the defeats of various Russian princes, defeats caused by the discord among them, speaks of Prince Vseslav's tragic last battle in the following terms:

> On the Nemiga the spread sheaves
> are heads,
> the flails that thresh
> are of steel,
> lives are laid out on the threshing floor,
> souls are winnowed from bodies.
> Nemiga's gory banks are not sowed goodly—
> sown with the bones of Russia's sons.

The Song of Igor's Campaign, trans. Vladimir Nabokov (New York: Vintage, 1960), 62.

8. The significance of this scene was first noted by George Steiner in his *Tolstoy or Dostoevsky: An Essay in the Old Criticism* (New York: Vintage, 1961), 86.

9. It was at Smolensk that the Russians had a chance to wage the first major battle against the French, but instead withdrew.

8. Dynamics and Building Blocks

1. This is how Tolstoy introduces Karataev to the reader: "Behind him [Pierre] in a stooping position sat a small man of whose presence he was first made aware by a strong smell of perspiration which came from him every time he moved" (*W&P*, 1073).

Notes and References

2. R. F. Christian, in a subtle discussion of Tolstoy's use of French, thinks that it is employed as a means of characterization. French phrases and sentences reveal their speakers' characters much more effectively, though subtly, than would their direct counterparts in Russian. In fact, many of these phrases have no Russian counterparts (Christian, 159ff.).

3. Morson, 74–75. For instance, Alexander Nikolaevich Radishchev (1749–1802) crowded the short story, the philosophical treatise, literary criticism, journalistic reporting, and epistolary prose under the single rubric of a travelogue entitled *Journey from St. Petersburg to Moscow* (1790).

4. Morson makes the same point: "Throughout the book, and especially in the battle scenes, Tolstoy juxtaposes sets of circumstances that present radically different possibilities at the same time, but in different places. The present is different not only from the immediate past and imminent future but also from the present that is happening only a few yards away. Time exists in pockets, hides in nooks, emerges suddenly from out of the smoke covering a part of the battlefield" (Morson, 168).

5. E. E. Zaidenshnur, "In Search of the Beginning of the Novel 'War and Peace,'" *Literaturnoe nasledstvo* (Literary heritage) 69 (1961): 294.

6. Saburov says that the basic motif of the majority of the early sketches for the novel is a review of contemporary political events given in the form of conversation among various characters (Saburov, 48).

7. This insight comes from a paper entitled "Memory, Attention and Imagination in Tolstoi," and presented by Natasha Sankovich of Stanford University, at the AAASS American Association for the Advancement of Slavic Studies conference, 5 February 1989.

8. See *W&P*, 228–30. Tolstoy, with his vicious but often well-hidden sense of humor, adds an irresistible touch here: Prince Vassily "embraced his daughter, then again Pierre, and kissed him with his malodorous mouth."

9. *W&P*, 1336. In a number of ways, though certainly not in its style, this train of Tolstoyan thought is reminiscent of Dostoyevski's Underground Man, who loudly clamors for the privilege "to stick his tongue out at the Crystal Palace," that is, at the set of universal laws predicting and determining human behavior. Fyodor Dostoyevski, *Notes from Underground* (Middlesex: Penguin Books, 1972) 33.

10. *W&P*, 1130. Tolstoy's doctor, Dushan Makovicky, attests that in 1905 Tolstoy read aloud to his company the story of a certain Decembrist Baten'kov, who had written a constitutional project in 1824 and had been jailed in solitary confinement for 19 years. This Baten'kov came to understand that his soul was free, and having realized this, he laughed so loudly that the guards ran over to see what was the matter (Makovicky, 147). If, as is quite likely, Tolstoy knew of this story before he wrote *War and Peace*, it

could have inspired the episode with Pierre. It is interesting to recall that Pierre was meant to become a Decembrist and be sent to Siberia.

9. Genre and the Hero

1. Scholars partial to this term include L. D. Opul'skaya, A. V. Chicherin, A. A. Saburov, V. Ermilov, and others.

2. L. D. Opul'skaya, *Roman-èpopoeia L. N. Tolstogo "Voina i mir"* (L. N. Tolstoy's novel-epos "War and Peace") (Moscow: Prosveshchenie, 1987), 139; hereafter cited in text as Opul'skaya.

3. Terras classifies the work through a broad inclusivity: "It is a sui generis combination of the psychological novel, the *Bildungsroman*, the family novel, and the historical novel, with a liberal admixture of the scope and tone of the epic" (Terras, 478).

4. Maksim Gorky, "Leo Tolstoy," *Sobranie sochinenij* (Collected works) (Moscow: State Belles Lettres Publishing House, 1963), vol. 18, 80.

5. George Steiner, "Tolstoy and Homer," in Harold Bloom, ed., *Modern Critical Views: Leo Tolstoy* (New York: Chelsea House, 1986), 73.

6. This particular tug-of-war is prefigured early in the novel, at Count Bezukhov's deathbed, when Princess Catiche physically struggles with Anna Mikhailovna over a briefcase, which, they presume, holds the count's will (*W&P*, 88–89).

7. Edward Wasiolek also notes that "in comparison with Andrey, Pierre is foolish, unattractive, naïve, and at times stupid." See Wasiolek, 84.

8. See *W&P*, 70: "'Do you know, that fat Pierre who sat opposite me is so funny!' said Natasha, stopping suddenly. 'I feel so happy.'" Pierre himself thought Natasha was a funny girl. There is quite a difference between the feelings of these two innocents and Andrey's thought, upon seeing Natasha: "Suddenly, he didn't know why, he felt a pang. The day was so beautiful, the sun so bright, everything around so gay, but that slim pretty girl did not know, or wish to know, of his existence" (*W&P*, 460).

9. Nonetheless, it is well worth noting that, as opposed to all these tall men with puny souls, Andrey is only of average height. Tolstoy objected when an illustrator of an early edition of the novel made Andrey "too tall." Letter to M. S. Bashilov, Nov. 12, 1865, *W&P*, 1360.

10. Nonetheless, it is possible to see in Pierre's great quest the faint outline of the traditional canon of saints' lives in medieval Russian literature. Pierre is a special child who comes into the world between great riches and illegitimacy; he has a deep and abiding interest in the meaning of life; he has a period of dissolute living and carousal; he is exposed to temptation in the figure of Hélène; he meets a messenger from above (Bazdeev); he attempts a

heroic deed that could have changed the world (killing Napoleon); he undergoes a period of incognito suffering in (French) captivity, followed by enlightenment. If Tolstoy had pursued his tale to its ultimate conclusion, one could imagine that Pierre the Decembrist would have achieved his martyrdom and apotheosis.

11. Richard E. Gustafson, *Leo Tolstoy, Resident and Stranger: A Study in Fiction and Theology* (Princeton, N.J.: Princeton University Press, 1986), 203.

Bibliography

Primary Sources

War and Peace. Edited by George Gibian and translated by Aylmer Maude. New York: W. W. Norton, 1966. This revised edition of Aylmer Maude's original publication (1922–23) contains many critical essays and sources.

Tolstoy's Diaries. Edited and translated by R. F. Christian. Vol. 1, 1847–94; vol. 2, 1895–1910. New York: Scribners, 1985. Extremely rich in various references to the works Tolstoy read and wrote.

L.N. Tolstoj o literature: Stat'i, pis'ma, dnevniki (L. N. Tolstoy on literature: Articles, letters, diaries). Edited by L. D. Gromova-Opul'skaya et al. Moscow: State Publishing House (Gosizdat), 1955. Tolstoy's statements on art, gleaned from his essays, diaries, and other sources.

Lev Tolstoj ob iskusstve i literature (Lev Tolstoy on art and literature). Edited by K. N. Lomunov. Vols. 1 and 2. Moscow: State Publishing House, 1958. An extensive collection arranged along topical lines.

L. N. Tolstoj, Perepiska s russkimi pisateljami (L. N. Tolstoy: Correspondence with Russian writers). Edited by S. Rozanova. Moscow: State Publishing House, 1962. Of particular interest is the correspondence with the Russian poet Afanasy Fet.

141

Secondary Sources

Works about Tolstoy

Bayley, John. *Tolstoy and the Novel*. New York: Viking, 1966. Perspicacious investigation of Tolstoy's achievement in relation to the genre of the novel.

Bocharov, S. C. *Roman Tolstogo "Voina i mir"* (Tolstoy's novel "War and Peace"). Moscow: State Belles Lettres Publishing House, 1978. Particularly good in observing both the major and minor components of the novel as equivalents in its total organization.

Bychkov, S. P., ed. *L. N. Tolstoy v russkoi kritike* (L. N. Tolstoy in Russian literary criticism). Moscow: State Belles Lettres Publishing House, 1952. Articles and excerpts from Russian critics about Tolstoy, with emphasis on authors from the nineteenth century.

Chicherin, A. V. *O yazykie i stile romana-èpopoeia L. N. Tolstogo 'Voina i mir'* (About the language and style of L. N. Tolstoy's novel-epopoeia "War and Peace"). L'vov, 1953. Rhetorical observations on Tolstoy's style.

Christian, R. F. *Tolstoy's "War and Peace": A Study*. Oxford: Clarendon Press, 1962. A penetrating study of Tolstoy's text, understood within the framework of a traditional novel.

Eikhenbaum, Boris. *Lev Tolstoy: Kniga pervaya* (Lev Tolstoy: Volume one). Leningrad: State Belles Lettres Publishing House, 1928.

———. *Lev Tolstoy: Kniga vtoraya* (Lev Tolstoy: Volume two). Leningrad: State Belles Lettres Publishing House, 1931. A particularly thorough historical investigation of all possible ideas that influenced Tolstoy as he was composing the novel. Also meticulously describes the process of writing the novel.

Ermilov, V. *Tolstoy—romanist* (Tolstoy the novelist). Moscow: State Belles Lettres Publishing House, 1965. Regards *War and Peace* as a "philosophical poem," but on the whole employs Soviet-style rhetoric, generalities, including the idea of class struggle as part of the epic dimension in the novel.

Gustafson, Richard. *Leo Tolstoy, Resident and Stranger: A Study in Fiction and Theology*. Princeton, N.J.: Princeton University Press, 1986. This standard-setting work is a fundamental investigation of Tolstoy's religious beliefs in relation to his art.

Jepsen, Laura. *From Achilles to Christ: The Myth of the Hero in Tolstoy's "War and Peace."* Author's publication, 1978. Offers some valuable insights into the concept of hero in the novel.

Bibliography

Kupreyanova, E. N. *O problematike i zhanrovoi prirode romana L. Tolstogo "Voina i mir"* (On the problematics and genre of L. N. Tolstoy's novel "War and Peace"). *Russkaja literatura* (Russian literature) 1 (1985), 161–172. Sober and scholarly account of the issues in literary theory pertaining to the concept and structure of genre, and its application to Tolstoy's book.

Lenin, V. I. *Tolstoy and His Time.* Moscow: International Publishers, 1952. A series of articles about Tolstoy's work that set the ideological markers for all subsequent Soviet literary criticism. No Soviet critic dared to claim any advance in understanding beyond Lenin's notion that Tolstoy, even as he unmasked society, was himself a patriarchal kulak in his mentality.

Literary Heritage 69 (1961); 75 (1965). Both volumes consist of a series of articles and documents pertaining to *War and Peace* and the period in which it was written.

Makovitsky, Dushan. *U Tolstogo.* Yasnopolyanskie zapiski A. P. Makovitskogo (At Tolstoy's: The Yasnaya Polyana notes of Dushan Makovitsky). 4 vols. Moscow: Science (Nauka), 1979. A humble and beautiful set of detailed notes of Tolstoy's daily life, his conversations, and his ideas by his personal doctor. Many of Tolstoy's recorded ideas can elucidate aspects of the novel.

Maude, Aylmer. *The Life of Tolstoy.* New York: Oxford University Press, 1987. A long and loving story of Tolstoy's life by his personal friend and translator.

Morson, Gary Saul. *Hidden in Plain View: Narrative and Creative Potentials in "War and Peace."* Stanford, Calif.: Stanford University Press, 1987. An erudite original look at the structure of *War and Peace.*

Opul'skaya, L. D. *Roman-èpopoeia L. N. Tostogo* (L. N. Tolstoy's novel-èpopoeia). Moscow: Prosveshchenie, 1987. A brief and somewhat rhetorical study, particularly good in its assessment of the emotional ambience of the novel.

Rowe, William W. *Leo Tolstoy.* Boston: Twayne, 1986. Some helpful notions concerning *War and Peace.*

Saburov, A. A. *"Voina i mir" L. N. Tolstogo: Problematika i poetika* (Lev Tolstoy's "War and Peace": Problematics and poetics). Moscow: Moscow University, 1959. Builds a very fine Soviet-style model, but not necessarily of Tolstoy's novel.

Shklovsky, Victor. *Lev Tolstoy.* Moscow: The Young Guard Publishing House, 1963. An imaginative, informed biography of Tolstoy, with useful commentaries on his works.

Silbajoris, Rimvydas. *Tolstoy's Aesthetics and His Art*. Columbus, Ohio: Slavica, 1991. Some comments on scenes in *War and Peace* in relation to Tolstoy's esthetics.

Simmons, Ernest J. *Leo Tolstoy*. Boston: Little, Brown & Co., 1946. An American classic in the field of Slavic studies, on par with the best nineteenth-century Russian biographical scholarship.

Sorokin, Boris. *Tolstoy in Prerevolutionary Russian Criticism*. Columbus: Ohio State University Press, 1979. A careful, sometimes original discussion of Russian critics of Tolstoy.

Wasiolek, Edward. *Tolstoy's Major Fiction*. Chicago, Ill.: University of Chicago Press, 1978. A convincing, insightful discussion.

Zaydenshnur, E. E. *"Voina i mir" L. N. Tolstogo: Sozdanie velikoj knigi* (Lev Tolstoy's "War and Peace": The creation of a great book). Moscow: Kniga [Book] Publishing House, 1966. Meticulous and intelligent retracing of the inception, birth, and growth of Tolstoy's novel.

General References

Berlin, Isaiah. *Russian Thinkers*. New York: Penguin, 1979. Contains the famous article on Tolstoy promoting the idea that Tolstoy was a hedgehog—someone who knows just one thing well— who wanted to be a fox—someone who is acquainted with a great many things.

Erlich, Victor. *Russian Formalism*. 'SGravenhage: Mouton, 1969. Still the best exposition of Russian formalist thought.

Freeborn, Richard. *The Rise of the Russian Novel*. Cambridge, England: Cambridge University Press, 1973. Contains interesting and refreshing commentary on *War and Peace*.

Steiner, George. *Tolstoy or Dostoevsky: An Essay in the Old Criticism*. New York: Vintage, 1961. Imaginative, argumentative, and elegant, this book is a profound look at the two Russian writers.

Terras, Victor, et al., eds. *Handbook of Russian Literature*. New Haven, Conn.: Yale University Press, 1985. An indispensable reference source for every library.

Index

Aksakov, Konstantin, 6
Alexander I, 102, 110–11
Anatoly Kuragin (character), 34, 40, 46, 47, 68, 80, 81, 87
Andrey Bolkonsky (character), 10, 14, 20, 53–54, 82–86, 100; at Battle of Borodino, 35, 67, 84, 101–2; death of, 37, 51, 60–61, 66, 67, 69, 83, 102, 133n3, 134nn5–6; as narrative voice, 60–62, 63, 69–71; and Natasha, 46–47, 117, 138n7; physical appearance, 138n8; and Pierre, 65–67, 69, 115, 116
Anna Scherer (character), 43, 50, 71–72, 73, 78, 100, 102, 133n1
Antecedents (of *War and Peace*), 29–31, 100–101
Anti-Westernism, 5, 8
Art, 12, 40, 46, 48, 106, 107; and morality, 19

Asmus, V. F., 22
Austerlitz, battle of, 13, 37, 60, 78, 85, 102, 116

Bagration (character), 63, 72–73, 93, 104
Bakhtin, Mikhail, 131n5
Baudelaire, Charles, 132n5
Bayley, John, 20, 25, 98
Beds, as symbol, 75–76, 78
Belinsky, Vissarion, 5
Berlin, Isaiah, 24
Bocharov, S., 8, 22, 114, 130n29
Borodino, battle of, 8, 40, 59, 77–78, 84, 89, 101, 133n3; Andrey's wounding at, 35, 67; described by Pierre, 98

Candle metaphor, 81, 84
Catherine II, 4, 6, 10
Causality, in history, 10, 74, 134n10; in the novel, 74–75

Characters, 31, 92–94, 97, 122;
    families, 33–34; minor, 8, 33,
    40, 43–50, 52, 56, 60, 63, 64,
    66, 68, 98, 100, 112, 114,
    119, 133n1, 11; physical traits
    of, 79; structural scheme of,
    24. See also Anatoly Kuragin,
    Andrey Bolkonsky, Anna
    Scherer, Bagration, Hélène
    Kuragin, Kutuzov, Lise
    Bolkonsky, Napoleon, Natasha
    Rostova, Nikolay Rostov,
    Pierre Bezukhov, Platon
    Karataev, Prince Nikolay
    Bolkonsky, Prince Vassily
    Kuragin, Princess Mary
    Bolkonsky
Chekov, Anton, 39
Chernyshevsky, Nikolai, 5, 17–18
Christian, R. F., 23, 35, 36, 96,
    108–9, 129n22, 137n2; on
    binary balance, 94; on dia-
    logue, 56; on recurrences, 79
Communication, 41–45, 53, 98; ver-
    sus miscommunication, 43
Consciousness: altered states of,
    67–68; of reality, 24–25
Cook, Albert, 77, 94, 99
Crimean War, 3, 31
Criticism (of War and Peace), 16–26,
    35–36
Culinary metaphor, 72

Dal, Vladimir: Proverbs of the
    Russian People, 133n2
Davie, Donald, 23
Death, 53, 66, 69, 84, 85, 102,
    116–17, 132n10; indifference
    of, 36–37; metaphors for, 13,
    82–84; and paradox, 14; of
    Petya, 48–50. See also Andrey
    Bolkonsky, death of

Decembrists, 5, 31, 109, 125n4
De Maistre, Joseph, 129n23
Dialogue, 56–57
Dichotomy, 38, 93, 94, 95–96
Diderot, Denis, 4
Digressions, 96
Dobrolyubov, Nikolai, 5
Don Quixote, 120
Door metaphor, 81–84, 85
Dostoyevski, Fyodor, 6–7, 18, 20,
    35, 126n6, 131n5, 137n9; The
    Brothers Karamazov, 7, 9;
    Crime and Punishment, 9,
    135n13; House of the Dead,
    127–28n8; The Possessed,
    135n13
Dreams, 49–50, 60, 99, 133n3

Eikhenbaum, Boris, 10, 16–17,
    21–22, 35–36, 109, 127n2; on
    origin of War and Peace, 32,
    95–96, 129n23
Empathy, 42–43
Encyclopedists, 88, 125n2
Epic (War and Peace as), 22–23, 25,
    91, 109–20
Ermilov, V., 86

Feet/legs, linkages of, 80–81
Fet, Afanasy, 17
Formalism, Russian, 21–22
Freeborn, Richard, 130n2
Freedom, 105–6, 122; individual,
    versus determinism, 10, 16,
    24, 55, 58, 106
Freemasonry, 64–65,
    134–35nn10–11, 135n3

Genre conventions, 16, 22, 35,
    110
Globe image, 50, 58, 69, 78,
    133n12, 133n3

Index

Gogol, Nikolay: *Dead Souls,* 9, 127–28n8; *Passages from a Correspondence with Friends,* 7
Goncharov, Ivan: *Oblomov,* 9
Gorky, Maxim, 110
Gustafson, Richard F., 122

Hélène Kuragin (character), 47–48, 79, 87–88, 93, 100, 104
Herzen, Alexander, 5
History, 5, 14, 17, 22, 97–99, 105; causality in, 10, 60, 134n10; and fiction, 10, 101; Tolstoy's philosophy of, 102, 106–7, 129n23

Identity, 21, 40
Interior monologue, 56
Irony, 8, 53, 60, 68, 77, 88–89, 94, 100

James, Henry, 23, 25, 92

Khomyakov, Aleksey, 6
Kireevsky, Ivan, 6
Kutuzov (character), 34, 40, 60, 93, 101, 104; physical characteristics of, 79, 89, 90; and retreat from Moscow, 103

Lay of the Host of Igor', 87, 136n7
Lenin, V. I., 20–21
Lermontov, Mikhail, 135n14; *Hero of Our Time,* 119
Lise Bolkonsky (character), 76, 79, 82–83
Lubbock, Percy, 23

"Making strange," 21, 46, 84, 129n20, 135–36n4; versus "making familiar," 44, 45

Makovicky, Dushan, 52, 137n10
Matlaw, Ralph, 95, 127n1
Maude, Aylmer, 11, 13, 22–23, 95, 134n8
Merezhkovsky, Dmitry, 19–20, 126n6
Mikhailovsky, N. K., 19, 128n11
Milton, John, 134n7
Mir, 8
Morson, Gary Saul, 25–26, 37–38, 57, 58, 83, 97, 121–22, 137n4
Moscow, 52, 67, 78

Napoleon, as character, 17, 43, 57, 59, 79, 81, 110–11, 115–16
Napoleonic Wars, 4–5, 8, 29, 89, 130n29
Narrative rhyming, 74–75, 90–91, 92
Narrative voice, 39, 41, 48, 55–57, 59–63, 65, 71, 73, 101, 102, 104
Natasha Rostova (character), 24, 25, 31, 33, 34, 37, 80–81, 117–18, 132nn7, 10; and death of Andrey, 68, 118; and Kuragin, 40, 46, 87, 118; at the opera, 46–48, 60; and Pierre, 85, 118; as symbol, 89–90, 118
Nature, 41–42, 65
Nikolay Rostov (character), 33, 37, 44–46, 58, 63, 79, 102
Novikov, Nikolay, 6

Opul'skaya, L. D., 22, 110
Organic principle, 37, 63
Origins (of *War and Peace*), 3

Paradox, 14, 19, 103, 105
Parody, 38, 52, 83, 97, 112, 113, 115, 121

Peter I, 4, 6
Pierre Bezukhov (character), 20, 24, 64, 100, 105, 115, 119–21, 138–39n9; and Andrey, 35, 53–54, 65–67, 69, 116; at Borodino, 35, 77–78, 98; as Decembrist, 5, 31; and dream, 50, 99, 133n3; and Freemasonry, 63, 64–65, 88, 120, 134nn9–11; and Natasha, 68, 85, 103, 115; physical appearance of, 79, 87, 114–15, 135n3
Platon Karataev (character), 8, 79, 93, 114, 122, 133nn1–3, 136n1; and proverbs, 58, 133n2
Pobedonostaev, Konstantin, 7
Pogodin, Mikhail P., 10, 129n23
Prayer, symbolism of, 89–90
Prince Nikolay Bolkonsky (character), 33, 46–47, 51, 61–62, 79, 80, 93; and couch, 75–76
Prince Vassily Kuragin (character), 43, 78, 80, 93, 100, 104
Princess Mary Bolkonsky (character), 33, 34, 51, 69, 75–76, 79, 80
Proudhon, Pierre, 10, 129n33
Proverbs, 58
Publication (of War and Peace), 32
Pushkin, Aleksandr: The Captain's Daughter, 10

Radishchev, Alexander, N., 137n3
Rahv, Philip, 25
Rational versus irrational, 19, 58
Realism, 22
Reality, 63; consciousness of, 24–25; reproduction of, 30, 41–42, 65, 91
Reflection, creation through, 40–42, 132n3

Rhetoric, 106
River, as metaphor, 53, 63, 69
Russia, 11, 16, 67, 89–90, 93; literary genre of, 17; Slavophilism in, 6–8; Soviet establishment in, 20–22; westernizing of, 4–8

Saburov, A., 10, 61, 137n6
Schöngraben, battle of, 62, 72, 78, 85
Shklovsky, Viktor, 21, 35, 74, 97, 99, 116, 133n12
Simplicity, art of, 25
Slavophilism, 6, 22
Sorokin, Boris, 128nn11, 12
Spinning metaphor, 71–72, 78
Steiner, George, 111, 136n8
Stendhal: The Charterhouse of Parma, 10
Strakhov, Nikolai N., 17, 36
Structural principles, 26, 32–33, 92–97

Terras, Victor, 109, 110, 115, 138n3
Threshing metaphor, 86–87
Time/space dimensions, 10, 31, 33, 53, 99
Tolstoy, Lev: Adolescence, 30; Anna Karenina, 14, 18, 122, 131n5; as anti-Western, 5–6, 132n4; as antihistorical, 17, 130n1; and Chekhov, 131n2; Childhood, 30, 130n3; and concept of freedom, 24 (see also Freedom); Confession, A, 134n8; Cossacks, The 31, 86; creativity, 122; Death of Ivan Ilyich, 14, 135n14, 135n2; "Hadzik Murat," 130n1; influences on, 10, 129n23;

Kreutzer Sonata, 14; Lenin on, 20–21, 128n15; on life, 15, 17; moral dimension in, 19–20, 22; and psychology, 18; "Raid, The," 133n11; *Sevastopol' Sketches,* 30; tension between intellect and intuition in, 19; "Three Deaths," 131n8; on time/space, 52–53; war, view of, 10, 30, 57, 61, 89, 130–31n4; *War and Peace,* view of, 3, 15–16, 109; "What Is Art?" 40; on writing, 12, 19, 126n4, 127–28n8

Turgenev, Ivan, 5, 9, 16, 125n5, 127n6

Urosov, Sergei S., 10–11, 36, 129n23, 131n7

Wasiolek, Edward, 23–24, 138n6
Waste, principle of, 25
Wild eyes metaphor, 87–89

Yasnaya Polyana, 3, 29–30, 101, 130n1, 135n2
Youth, 30

Zaidenshnur, E., 22, 100

The Author

Rimvydas Silbajoris taught Russian literature and language at Oberlin College and The Ohio State University until his retirement in 1991. Born in Lithuania, he came to the United States in 1949 and earned a B.A. in English in 1953 from Antioch College, an M.A. in Russian in 1955 from Columbia University, and a Ph.D. in Russian in 1962, also from Columbia. Silbajoris has written extensively on Lithuanian and Russian prose and poetry, and is the author of books on Russian versification in the eighteenth century, the aesthetics of Leo Tolstoy, as well as several monographs on Lithuanian topics.